C-984   CAREER EXAMINATION SERIES

*This is your
PASSBOOK for...*

Public Health Sanitarian Trainee

*Test Preparation Study Guide
Questions & Answers*

COPYRIGHT NOTICE

This book is SOLELY intended for, is sold ONLY to, and its use is RESTRICTED to individual, bona fide applicants or candidates who qualify by virtue of having seriously filed applications for appropriate license, certificate, professional and/or promotional advancement, higher school matriculation, scholarship, or other legitimate requirements of education and/or governmental authorities.

This book is NOT intended for use, class instruction, tutoring, training, duplication, copying, reprinting, excerption, or adaptation, etc., by:

1) Other publishers
2) Proprietors and/or Instructors of "Coaching" and/or Preparatory Courses
3) Personnel and/or Training Divisions of commercial, industrial, and governmental organizations
4) Schools, colleges, or universities and/or their departments and staffs, including teachers and other personnel
5) Testing Agencies or Bureaus
6) Study groups which seek by the purchase of a single volume to copy and/or duplicate and/or adapt this material for use by the group as a whole without having purchased individual volumes for each of the members of the group
7) Et al.

Such persons would be in violation of appropriate Federal and State statutes.

PROVISION OF LICENSING AGREEMENTS – Recognized educational, commercial, industrial, and governmental institutions and organizations, and others legitimately engaged in educational pursuits, including training, testing, and measurement activities, may address request for a licensing agreement to the copyright owners, who will determine whether, and under what conditions, including fees and charges, the materials in this book may be used them. In other words, a licensing facility exists for the legitimate use of the material in this book on other than an individual basis. However, it is asseverated and affirmed here that the material in this book CANNOT be used without the receipt of the express permission of such a licensing agreement from the Publishers. Inquiries re licensing should be addressed to the company, attention rights and permissions department.

All rights reserved, including the right of reproduction in whole or in part, in any form or by any means, electronic or mechanical, including photocopying, recording, or by any information storage and retrieval system, without permission in writing from the Publisher.

Copyright © 2024 by
National Learning Corporation

212 Michael Drive, Syosset, NY 11791
(516) 921-8888 • www.passbooks.com
E-mail: info@passbooks.com

PASSBOOK® SERIES

THE *PASSBOOK® SERIES* has been created to prepare applicants and candidates for the ultimate academic battlefield – the examination room.

At some time in our lives, each and every one of us may be required to take an examination – for validation, matriculation, admission, qualification, registration, certification, or licensure.

Based on the assumption that every applicant or candidate has met the basic formal educational standards, has taken the required number of courses, and read the necessary texts, the *PASSBOOK® SERIES* furnishes the one special preparation which may assure passing with confidence, instead of failing with insecurity. Examination questions – together with answers – are furnished as the basic vehicle for study so that the mysteries of the examination and its compounding difficulties may be eliminated or diminished by a sure method.

This book is meant to help you pass your examination provided that you qualify and are serious in your objective.

The entire field is reviewed through the huge store of content information which is succinctly presented through a provocative and challenging approach – the question-and-answer method.

A climate of success is established by furnishing the correct answers at the end of each test.

You soon learn to recognize types of questions, forms of questions, and patterns of questioning. You may even begin to anticipate expected outcomes.

You perceive that many questions are repeated or adapted so that you can gain acute insights, which may enable you to score many sure points.

You learn how to confront new questions, or types of questions, and to attack them confidently and work out the correct answers.

You note objectives and emphases, and recognize pitfalls and dangers, so that you may make positive educational adjustments.

Moreover, you are kept fully informed in relation to new concepts, methods, practices, and directions in the field.

You discover that you are actually taking the examination all the time: you are preparing for the examination by "taking" an examination, not by reading extraneous and/or supererogatory textbooks.

In short, this PASSBOOK®, used directedly, should be an important factor in helping you to pass your test.

PUBLIC HEALTH SANITARIAN TRAINEE

DUTIES
Assists in executing and enforcing the provisions of the Public Health Law, Sanitary Codes, and State Environmental Conservation Law, while undergoing on-the-job training to become qualified as a Public Health Sanitarian. Participates in the disposal systems, bathing beaches and swimming pools, facilities for refuse disposal, x-ray installations, temporary residences, farm labor camps, air pollution control devices, sewage and industrial waste treatment plants, toxic materials storage facilities, water supply and marine monitoring. Collects water, food and other required samples for laboratory examination. Performs and submits reports on investigations and field inspections. Does related duties as required.

SCOPE OF THE EXAMINATION
The multiple-choice written test will cover knowledge, skills, and/or abilities in such areas as:
1. Reading comprehension and interpreting quasi-legal passages;
2. Preparation of written material;
3. Science with emphasis on chemistry and biology; and
4. Selecting proper course of action (judgment).

HOW TO TAKE A TEST

I. YOU MUST PASS AN EXAMINATION

A. WHAT EVERY CANDIDATE SHOULD KNOW
Examination applicants often ask us for help in preparing for the written test. What can I study in advance? What kinds of questions will be asked? How will the test be given? How will the papers be graded?

As an applicant for a civil service examination, you may be wondering about some of these things. Our purpose here is to suggest effective methods of advance study and to describe civil service examinations.

Your chances for success on this examination can be increased if you know how to prepare. Those "pre-examination jitters" can be reduced if you know what to expect. You can even experience an adventure in good citizenship if you know why civil service exams are given.

B. WHY ARE CIVIL SERVICE EXAMINATIONS GIVEN?
Civil service examinations are important to you in two ways. As a citizen, you want public jobs filled by employees who know how to do their work. As a job seeker, you want a fair chance to compete for that job on an equal footing with other candidates. The best-known means of accomplishing this two-fold goal is the competitive examination.

Exams are widely publicized throughout the nation. They may be administered for jobs in federal, state, city, municipal, town or village governments or agencies.

Any citizen may apply, with some limitations, such as the age or residence of applicants. Your experience and education may be reviewed to see whether you meet the requirements for the particular examination. When these requirements exist, they are reasonable and applied consistently to all applicants. Thus, a competitive examination may cause you some uneasiness now, but it is your privilege and safeguard.

C. HOW ARE CIVIL SERVICE EXAMS DEVELOPED?
Examinations are carefully written by trained technicians who are specialists in the field known as "psychological measurement," in consultation with recognized authorities in the field of work that the test will cover. These experts recommend the subject matter areas or skills to be tested; only those knowledges or skills important to your success on the job are included. The most reliable books and source materials available are used as references. Together, the experts and technicians judge the difficulty level of the questions.

Test technicians know how to phrase questions so that the problem is clearly stated. Their ethics do not permit "trick" or "catch" questions. Questions may have been tried out on sample groups, or subjected to statistical analysis, to determine their usefulness.

Written tests are often used in combination with performance tests, ratings of training and experience, and oral interviews. All of these measures combine to form the best-known means of finding the right person for the right job.

II. HOW TO PASS THE WRITTEN TEST

A. NATURE OF THE EXAMINATION

To prepare intelligently for civil service examinations, you should know how they differ from school examinations you have taken. In school you were assigned certain definite pages to read or subjects to cover. The examination questions were quite detailed and usually emphasized memory. Civil service exams, on the other hand, try to discover your present ability to perform the duties of a position, plus your potentiality to learn these duties. In other words, a civil service exam attempts to predict how successful you will be. Questions cover such a broad area that they cannot be as minute and detailed as school exam questions.

In the public service similar kinds of work, or positions, are grouped together in one "class." This process is known as *position-classification*. All the positions in a class are paid according to the salary range for that class. One class title covers all of these positions, and they are all tested by the same examination.

B. FOUR BASIC STEPS

1) Study the announcement

How, then, can you know what subjects to study? Our best answer is: "Learn as much as possible about the class of positions for which you've applied." The exam will test the knowledge, skills and abilities needed to do the work.

Your most valuable source of information about the position you want is the official exam announcement. This announcement lists the training and experience qualifications. Check these standards and apply only if you come reasonably close to meeting them.

The brief description of the position in the examination announcement offers some clues to the subjects which will be tested. Think about the job itself. Review the duties in your mind. Can you perform them, or are there some in which you are rusty? Fill in the blank spots in your preparation.

Many jurisdictions preview the written test in the exam announcement by including a section called "Knowledge and Abilities Required," "Scope of the Examination," or some similar heading. Here you will find out specifically what fields will be tested.

2) Review your own background

Once you learn in general what the position is all about, and what you need to know to do the work, ask yourself which subjects you already know fairly well and which need improvement. You may wonder whether to concentrate on improving your strong areas or on building some background in your fields of weakness. When the announcement has specified "some knowledge" or "considerable knowledge," or has used adjectives like "beginning principles of…" or "advanced … methods," you can get a clue as to the number and difficulty of questions to be asked in any given field. More questions, and hence broader coverage, would be included for those subjects which are more important in the work. Now weigh your strengths and weaknesses against the job requirements and prepare accordingly.

3) Determine the level of the position

Another way to tell how intensively you should prepare is to understand the level of the job for which you are applying. Is it the entering level? In other words, is this the position in which beginners in a field of work are hired? Or is it an intermediate or advanced level? Sometimes this is indicated by such words as "Junior" or "Senior" in the class title. Other jurisdictions use Roman numerals to designate the level – Clerk I, Clerk II, for example. The word "Supervisor" sometimes appears in the title. If the level is not indicated by the title, check the description of duties. Will you be working under very close supervision, or will you have responsibility for independent decisions in this work?

4) Choose appropriate study materials

Now that you know the subjects to be examined and the relative amount of each subject to be covered, you can choose suitable study materials. For beginning level jobs, or even advanced ones, if you have a pronounced weakness in some aspect of your training, read a modern, standard textbook in that field. Be sure it is up to date and has general coverage. Such books are normally available at your library, and the librarian will be glad to help you locate one. For entry-level positions, questions of appropriate difficulty are chosen – neither highly advanced questions, nor those too simple. Such questions require careful thought but not advanced training.

If the position for which you are applying is technical or advanced, you will read more advanced, specialized material. If you are already familiar with the basic principles of your field, elementary textbooks would waste your time. Concentrate on advanced textbooks and technical periodicals. Think through the concepts and review difficult problems in your field.

These are all general sources. You can get more ideas on your own initiative, following these leads. For example, training manuals and publications of the government agency which employs workers in your field can be useful, particularly for technical and professional positions. A letter or visit to the government department involved may result in more specific study suggestions, and certainly will provide you with a more definite idea of the exact nature of the position you are seeking.

III. KINDS OF TESTS

Tests are used for purposes other than measuring knowledge and ability to perform specified duties. For some positions, it is equally important to test ability to make adjustments to new situations or to profit from training. In others, basic mental abilities not dependent on information are essential. Questions which test these things may not appear as pertinent to the duties of the position as those which test for knowledge and information. Yet they are often highly important parts of a fair examination. For very general questions, it is almost impossible to help you direct your study efforts. What we can do is to point out some of the more common of these general abilities needed in public service positions and describe some typical questions.

1) General information

Broad, general information has been found useful for predicting job success in some kinds of work. This is tested in a variety of ways, from vocabulary lists to questions about current events. Basic background in some field of work, such as sociology or economics, may be sampled in a group of questions. Often these are principles which have become familiar to most persons through exposure rather than through formal training. It is difficult to advise you how to study for these questions; being alert to the world around you is our best suggestion.

2) Verbal ability

An example of an ability needed in many positions is verbal or language ability. Verbal ability is, in brief, the ability to use and understand words. Vocabulary and grammar tests are typical measures of this ability. Reading comprehension or paragraph interpretation questions are common in many kinds of civil service tests. You are given a paragraph of written material and asked to find its central meaning.

3) Numerical ability

Number skills can be tested by the familiar arithmetic problem, by checking paired lists of numbers to see which are alike and which are different, or by interpreting charts and graphs. In the latter test, a graph may be printed in the test booklet which you are asked to use as the basis for answering questions.

4) Observation

A popular test for law-enforcement positions is the observation test. A picture is shown to you for several minutes, then taken away. Questions about the picture test your ability to observe both details and larger elements.

5) Following directions

In many positions in the public service, the employee must be able to carry out written instructions dependably and accurately. You may be given a chart with several columns, each column listing a variety of information. The questions require you to carry out directions involving the information given in the chart.

6) Skills and aptitudes

Performance tests effectively measure some manual skills and aptitudes. When the skill is one in which you are trained, such as typing or shorthand, you can practice. These tests are often very much like those given in business school or high school courses. For many of the other skills and aptitudes, however, no short-time preparation can be made. Skills and abilities natural to you or that you have developed throughout your lifetime are being tested.

Many of the general questions just described provide all the data needed to answer the questions and ask you to use your reasoning ability to find the answers. Your best preparation for these tests, as well as for tests of facts and ideas, is to be at your physical and mental best. You, no doubt, have your own methods of getting into an exam-taking mood and keeping "in shape." The next section lists some ideas on this subject.

IV. KINDS OF QUESTIONS

Only rarely is the "essay" question, which you answer in narrative form, used in civil service tests. Civil service tests are usually of the short-answer type. Full instructions for answering these questions will be given to you at the examination. But in case this is your first experience with short-answer questions and separate answer sheets, here is what you need to know:

1) Multiple-choice Questions

Most popular of the short-answer questions is the "multiple choice" or "best answer" question. It can be used, for example, to test for factual knowledge, ability to solve problems or judgment in meeting situations found at work.

A multiple-choice question is normally one of three types—
- It can begin with an incomplete statement followed by several possible endings. You are to find the one ending which *best* completes the statement, although some of the others may not be entirely wrong.
- It can also be a complete statement in the form of a question which is answered by choosing one of the statements listed.

- It can be in the form of a problem – again you select the best answer.

Here is an example of a multiple-choice question with a discussion which should give you some clues as to the method for choosing the right answer:

When an employee has a complaint about his assignment, the action which will *best* help him overcome his difficulty is to
- A. discuss his difficulty with his coworkers
- B. take the problem to the head of the organization
- C. take the problem to the person who gave him the assignment
- D. say nothing to anyone about his complaint

In answering this question, you should study each of the choices to find which is best. Consider choice "A" – Certainly an employee may discuss his complaint with fellow employees, but no change or improvement can result, and the complaint remains unresolved. Choice "B" is a poor choice since the head of the organization probably does not know what assignment you have been given, and taking your problem to him is known as "going over the head" of the supervisor. The supervisor, or person who made the assignment, is the person who can clarify it or correct any injustice. Choice "C" is, therefore, correct. To say nothing, as in choice "D," is unwise. Supervisors have and interest in knowing the problems employees are facing, and the employee is seeking a solution to his problem.

2) True/False Questions

The "true/false" or "right/wrong" form of question is sometimes used. Here a complete statement is given. Your job is to decide whether the statement is right or wrong.

SAMPLE: A roaming cell-phone call to a nearby city costs less than a non-roaming call to a distant city.

This statement is wrong, or false, since roaming calls are more expensive.

This is not a complete list of all possible question forms, although most of the others are variations of these common types. You will always get complete directions for answering questions. Be sure you understand *how* to mark your answers – ask questions until you do.

V. RECORDING YOUR ANSWERS

Computer terminals are used more and more today for many different kinds of exams.

For an examination with very few applicants, you may be told to record your answers in the test booklet itself. Separate answer sheets are much more common. If this separate answer sheet is to be scored by machine – and this is often the case – it is highly important that you mark your answers correctly in order to get credit.

An electronic scoring machine is often used in civil service offices because of the speed with which papers can be scored. Machine-scored answer sheets must be marked with a pencil, which will be given to you. This pencil has a high graphite content which responds to the electronic scoring machine. As a matter of fact, stray dots may register as answers, so do not let your pencil rest on the answer sheet while you are pondering the correct answer. Also, if your pencil lead breaks or is otherwise defective, ask for another.

Since the answer sheet will be dropped in a slot in the scoring machine, be careful not to bend the corners or get the paper crumpled.

The answer sheet normally has five vertical columns of numbers, with 30 numbers to a column. These numbers correspond to the question numbers in your test booklet. After each number, going across the page are four or five pairs of dotted lines. These short dotted lines have small letters or numbers above them. The first two pairs may also have a "T" or "F" above the letters. This indicates that the first two pairs only are to be used if the questions are of the true-false type. If the questions are multiple choice, disregard the "T" and "F" and pay attention only to the small letters or numbers.

Answer your questions in the manner of the sample that follows:

32. The largest city in the United States is
    A. Washington, D.C.
    B. New York City
    C. Chicago
    D. Detroit
    E. San Francisco

1) Choose the answer you think is best. (New York City is the largest, so "B" is correct.)
2) Find the row of dotted lines numbered the same as the question you are answering. (Find row number 32)
3) Find the pair of dotted lines corresponding to the answer. (Find the pair of lines under the mark "B.")
4) Make a solid black mark between the dotted lines.

VI. BEFORE THE TEST

Common sense will help you find procedures to follow to get ready for an examination. Too many of us, however, overlook these sensible measures. Indeed, nervousness and fatigue have been found to be the most serious reasons why applicants fail to do their best on civil service tests. Here is a list of reminders:

- Begin your preparation early – Don't wait until the last minute to go scurrying around for books and materials or to find out what the position is all about.
- Prepare continuously – An hour a night for a week is better than an all-night cram session. This has been definitely established. What is more, a night a week for a month will return better dividends than crowding your study into a shorter period of time.
- Locate the place of the exam – You have been sent a notice telling you when and where to report for the examination. If the location is in a different town or otherwise unfamiliar to you, it would be well to inquire the best route and learn something about the building.
- Relax the night before the test – Allow your mind to rest. Do not study at all that night. Plan some mild recreation or diversion; then go to bed early and get a good night's sleep.
- Get up early enough to make a leisurely trip to the place for the test – This way unforeseen events, traffic snarls, unfamiliar buildings, etc. will not upset you.
- Dress comfortably – A written test is not a fashion show. You will be known by number and not by name, so wear something comfortable.

- Leave excess paraphernalia at home – Shopping bags and odd bundles will get in your way. You need bring only the items mentioned in the official notice you received; usually everything you need is provided. Do not bring reference books to the exam. They will only confuse those last minutes and be taken away from you when in the test room.
- Arrive somewhat ahead of time – If because of transportation schedules you must get there very early, bring a newspaper or magazine to take your mind off yourself while waiting.
- Locate the examination room – When you have found the proper room, you will be directed to the seat or part of the room where you will sit. Sometimes you are given a sheet of instructions to read while you are waiting. Do not fill out any forms until you are told to do so; just read them and be prepared.
- Relax and prepare to listen to the instructions
- If you have any physical problem that may keep you from doing your best, be sure to tell the test administrator. If you are sick or in poor health, you really cannot do your best on the exam. You can come back and take the test some other time.

VII. AT THE TEST

The day of the test is here and you have the test booklet in your hand. The temptation to get going is very strong. Caution! There is more to success than knowing the right answers. You must know how to identify your papers and understand variations in the type of short-answer question used in this particular examination. Follow these suggestions for maximum results from your efforts:

1) Cooperate with the monitor

The test administrator has a duty to create a situation in which you can be as much at ease as possible. He will give instructions, tell you when to begin, check to see that you are marking your answer sheet correctly, and so on. He is not there to guard you, although he will see that your competitors do not take unfair advantage. He wants to help you do your best.

2) Listen to all instructions

Don't jump the gun! Wait until you understand all directions. In most civil service tests you get more time than you need to answer the questions. So don't be in a hurry. Read each word of instructions until you clearly understand the meaning. Study the examples, listen to all announcements and follow directions. Ask questions if you do not understand what to do.

3) Identify your papers

Civil service exams are usually identified by number only. You will be assigned a number; you must not put your name on your test papers. Be sure to copy your number correctly. Since more than one exam may be given, copy your exact examination title.

4) Plan your time

Unless you are told that a test is a "speed" or "rate of work" test, speed itself is usually not important. Time enough to answer all the questions will be provided, but this does not mean that you have all day. An overall time limit has been set. Divide the total time (in minutes) by the number of questions to determine the approximate time you have for each question.

5) Do not linger over difficult questions

If you come across a difficult question, mark it with a paper clip (useful to have along) and come back to it when you have been through the booklet. One caution if you do this – be sure to skip a number on your answer sheet as well. Check often to be sure that you have not lost your place and that you are marking in the row numbered the same as the question you are answering.

6) Read the questions

Be sure you know what the question asks! Many capable people are unsuccessful because they failed to *read* the questions correctly.

7) Answer all questions

Unless you have been instructed that a penalty will be deducted for incorrect answers, it is better to guess than to omit a question.

8) Speed tests

It is often better NOT to guess on speed tests. It has been found that on timed tests people are tempted to spend the last few seconds before time is called in marking answers at random – without even reading them – in the hope of picking up a few extra points. To discourage this practice, the instructions may warn you that your score will be "corrected" for guessing. That is, a penalty will be applied. The incorrect answers will be deducted from the correct ones, or some other penalty formula will be used.

9) Review your answers

If you finish before time is called, go back to the questions you guessed or omitted to give them further thought. Review other answers if you have time.

10) Return your test materials

If you are ready to leave before others have finished or time is called, take ALL your materials to the monitor and leave quietly. Never take any test material with you. The monitor can discover whose papers are not complete, and taking a test booklet may be grounds for disqualification.

VIII. EXAMINATION TECHNIQUES

1) Read the general instructions carefully. These are usually printed on the first page of the exam booklet. As a rule, these instructions refer to the timing of the examination; the fact that you should not start work until the signal and must stop work at a signal, etc. If there are any *special* instructions, such as a choice of questions to be answered, make sure that you note this instruction carefully.

2) When you are ready to start work on the examination, that is as soon as the signal has been given, read the instructions to each question booklet, underline any key words or phrases, such as *least, best, outline, describe* and the like. In this way you will tend to answer as requested rather than discover on reviewing your paper that you *listed without describing*, that you selected the *worst* choice rather than the *best* choice, etc.

3) If the examination is of the objective or multiple-choice type – that is, each question will also give a series of possible answers: A, B, C or D, and you are called upon to select the best answer and write the letter next to that answer on your answer paper – it is advisable to start answering each question in turn. There may be anywhere from 50 to 100 such questions in the three or four hours allotted and you can see how much time would be taken if you read through all the questions before beginning to answer any. Furthermore, if you come across a question or group of questions which you know would be difficult to answer, it would undoubtedly affect your handling of all the other questions.

4) If the examination is of the essay type and contains but a few questions, it is a moot point as to whether you should read all the questions before starting to answer any one. Of course, if you are given a choice – say five out of seven and the like – then it is essential to read all the questions so you can eliminate the two that are most difficult. If, however, you are asked to answer all the questions, there may be danger in trying to answer the easiest one first because you may find that you will spend too much time on it. The best technique is to answer the first question, then proceed to the second, etc.

5) Time your answers. Before the exam begins, write down the time it started, then add the time allowed for the examination and write down the time it must be completed, then divide the time available somewhat as follows:
   - If 3-1/2 hours are allowed, that would be 210 minutes. If you have 80 objective-type questions, that would be an average of 2-1/2 minutes per question. Allow yourself no more than 2 minutes per question, or a total of 160 minutes, which will permit about 50 minutes to review.
   - If for the time allotment of 210 minutes there are 7 essay questions to answer, that would average about 30 minutes a question. Give yourself only 25 minutes per question so that you have about 35 minutes to review.

6) The most important instruction is to *read each question* and make sure you know what is wanted. The second most important instruction is to *time yourself properly* so that you answer every question. The third most important instruction is to *answer every question*. Guess if you have to but include something for each question. Remember that you will receive no credit for a blank and will probably receive some credit if you write something in answer to an essay question. If you guess a letter – say "B" for a multiple-choice question – you may have guessed right. If you leave a blank as an answer to a multiple-choice question, the examiners may respect your feelings but it will not add a point to your score. Some exams may penalize you for wrong answers, so in such cases *only*, you may not want to guess unless you have some basis for your answer.

7) Suggestions
   a. Objective-type questions
      1. Examine the question booklet for proper sequence of pages and questions
      2. Read all instructions carefully
      3. Skip any question which seems too difficult; return to it after all other questions have been answered
      4. Apportion your time properly; do not spend too much time on any single question or group of questions

5. Note and underline key words – *all, most, fewest, least, best, worst, same, opposite,* etc.
6. Pay particular attention to negatives
7. Note unusual option, e.g., unduly long, short, complex, different or similar in content to the body of the question
8. Observe the use of "hedging" words – *probably, may, most likely,* etc.
9. Make sure that your answer is put next to the same number as the question
10. Do not second-guess unless you have good reason to believe the second answer is definitely more correct
11. Cross out original answer if you decide another answer is more accurate; do not erase until you are ready to hand your paper in
12. Answer all questions; guess unless instructed otherwise
13. Leave time for review

   b. Essay questions
1. Read each question carefully
2. Determine exactly what is wanted. Underline key words or phrases.
3. Decide on outline or paragraph answer
4. Include many different points and elements unless asked to develop any one or two points or elements
5. Show impartiality by giving pros and cons unless directed to select one side only
6. Make and write down any assumptions you find necessary to answer the questions
7. Watch your English, grammar, punctuation and choice of words
8. Time your answers; don't crowd material

8) Answering the essay question

Most essay questions can be answered by framing the specific response around several key words or ideas. Here are a few such key words or ideas:

M's: manpower, materials, methods, money, management
P's: purpose, program, policy, plan, procedure, practice, problems, pitfalls, personnel, public relations

   a. Six basic steps in handling problems:
1. Preliminary plan and background development
2. Collect information, data and facts
3. Analyze and interpret information, data and facts
4. Analyze and develop solutions as well as make recommendations
5. Prepare report and sell recommendations
6. Install recommendations and follow up effectiveness

   b. Pitfalls to avoid
1. *Taking things for granted* – A statement of the situation does not necessarily imply that each of the elements is necessarily true; for example, a complaint may be invalid and biased so that all that can be taken for granted is that a complaint has been registered

2. *Considering only one side of a situation* – Wherever possible, indicate several alternatives and then point out the reasons you selected the best one
3. *Failing to indicate follow up* – Whenever your answer indicates action on your part, make certain that you will take proper follow-up action to see how successful your recommendations, procedures or actions turn out to be
4. *Taking too long in answering any single question* – Remember to time your answers properly

IX. AFTER THE TEST

Scoring procedures differ in detail among civil service jurisdictions although the general principles are the same. Whether the papers are hand-scored or graded by machine we have described, they are nearly always graded by number. That is, the person who marks the paper knows only the number – never the name – of the applicant. Not until all the papers have been graded will they be matched with names. If other tests, such as training and experience or oral interview ratings have been given, scores will be combined. Different parts of the examination usually have different weights. For example, the written test might count 60 percent of the final grade, and a rating of training and experience 40 percent. In many jurisdictions, veterans will have a certain number of points added to their grades.

After the final grade has been determined, the names are placed in grade order and an eligible list is established. There are various methods for resolving ties between those who get the same final grade – probably the most common is to place first the name of the person whose application was received first. Job offers are made from the eligible list in the order the names appear on it. You will be notified of your grade and your rank as soon as all these computations have been made. This will be done as rapidly as possible.

People who are found to meet the requirements in the announcement are called "eligibles." Their names are put on a list of eligible candidates. An eligible's chances of getting a job depend on how high he stands on this list and how fast agencies are filling jobs from the list.

When a job is to be filled from a list of eligibles, the agency asks for the names of people on the list of eligibles for that job. When the civil service commission receives this request, it sends to the agency the names of the three people highest on this list. Or, if the job to be filled has specialized requirements, the office sends the agency the names of the top three persons who meet these requirements from the general list.

The appointing officer makes a choice from among the three people whose names were sent to him. If the selected person accepts the appointment, the names of the others are put back on the list to be considered for future openings.

That is the rule in hiring from all kinds of eligible lists, whether they are for typist, carpenter, chemist, or something else. For every vacancy, the appointing officer has his choice of any one of the top three eligibles on the list. This explains why the person whose name is on top of the list sometimes does not get an appointment when some of the persons lower on the list do. If the appointing officer chooses the second or third eligible, the No. 1 eligible does not get a job at once, but stays on the list until he is appointed or the list is terminated.

X. HOW TO PASS THE INTERVIEW TEST

The examination for which you applied requires an oral interview test. You have already taken the written test and you are now being called for the interview test – the final part of the formal examination.

You may think that it is not possible to prepare for an interview test and that there are no procedures to follow during an interview. Our purpose is to point out some things you can do in advance that will help you and some good rules to follow and pitfalls to avoid while you are being interviewed.

What is an interview supposed to test?

The written examination is designed to test the technical knowledge and competence of the candidate; the oral is designed to evaluate intangible qualities, not readily measured otherwise, and to establish a list showing the relative fitness of each candidate – as measured against his competitors – for the position sought. Scoring is not on the basis of "right" and "wrong," but on a sliding scale of values ranging from "not passable" to "outstanding." As a matter of fact, it is possible to achieve a relatively low score without a single "incorrect" answer because of evident weakness in the qualities being measured.

Occasionally, an examination may consist entirely of an oral test – either an individual or a group oral. In such cases, information is sought concerning the technical knowledges and abilities of the candidate, since there has been no written examination for this purpose. More commonly, however, an oral test is used to supplement a written examination.

Who conducts interviews?

The composition of oral boards varies among different jurisdictions. In nearly all, a representative of the personnel department serves as chairman. One of the members of the board may be a representative of the department in which the candidate would work. In some cases, "outside experts" are used, and, frequently, a businessman or some other representative of the general public is asked to serve. Labor and management or other special groups may be represented. The aim is to secure the services of experts in the appropriate field.

However the board is composed, it is a good idea (and not at all improper or unethical) to ascertain in advance of the interview who the members are and what groups they represent. When you are introduced to them, you will have some idea of their backgrounds and interests, and at least you will not stutter and stammer over their names.

What should be done before the interview?

While knowledge about the board members is useful and takes some of the surprise element out of the interview, there is other preparation which is more substantive. It *is* possible to prepare for an oral interview – in several ways:

1) Keep a copy of your application and review it carefully before the interview

This may be the only document before the oral board, and the starting point of the interview. Know what education and experience you have listed there, and the sequence and dates of all of it. Sometimes the board will ask you to review the highlights of your experience for them; you should not have to hem and haw doing it.

2) Study the class specification and the examination announcement

Usually, the oral board has one or both of these to guide them. The qualities, characteristics or knowledges required by the position sought are stated in these documents. They offer valuable clues as to the nature of the oral interview. For example, if the job involves supervisory responsibilities, the announcement will usually indicate that knowledge of modern supervisory methods and the qualifications of the candidate as a supervisor will be tested. If so, you can expect such questions, frequently in the form of a hypothetical situation which you are expected to solve. NEVER go into an oral without knowledge of the duties and responsibilities of the job you seek.

3) Think through each qualification required

Try to visualize the kind of questions you would ask if you were a board member. How well could you answer them? Try especially to appraise your own knowledge and background in each area, *measured against the job sought*, and identify any areas in which you are weak. Be critical and realistic – do not flatter yourself.

4) Do some general reading in areas in which you feel you may be weak

For example, if the job involves supervision and your past experience has NOT, some general reading in supervisory methods and practices, particularly in the field of human relations, might be useful. Do NOT study agency procedures or detailed manuals. The oral board will be testing your understanding and capacity, not your memory.

5) Get a good night's sleep and watch your general health and mental attitude

You will want a clear head at the interview. Take care of a cold or any other minor ailment, and of course, no hangovers.

What should be done on the day of the interview?

Now comes the day of the interview itself. Give yourself plenty of time to get there. Plan to arrive somewhat ahead of the scheduled time, particularly if your appointment is in the fore part of the day. If a previous candidate fails to appear, the board might be ready for you a bit early. By early afternoon an oral board is almost invariably behind schedule if there are many candidates, and you may have to wait. Take along a book or magazine to read, or your application to review, but leave any extraneous material in the waiting room when you go in for your interview. In any event, relax and compose yourself.

The matter of dress is important. The board is forming impressions about you – from your experience, your manners, your attitude, and your appearance. Give your personal appearance careful attention. Dress your best, but not your flashiest. Choose conservative, appropriate clothing, and be sure it is immaculate. This is a business interview, and your appearance should indicate that you regard it as such. Besides, being well groomed and properly dressed will help boost your confidence.

Sooner or later, someone will call your name and escort you into the interview room. *This is it.* From here on you are on your own. It is too late for any more preparation. But remember, you asked for this opportunity to prove your fitness, and you are here because your request was granted.

What happens when you go in?

The usual sequence of events will be as follows: The clerk (who is often the board stenographer) will introduce you to the chairman of the oral board, who will introduce you to the other members of the board. Acknowledge the introductions before you sit down. Do not be surprised if you find a microphone facing you or a stenotypist sitting by. Oral interviews are usually recorded in the event of an appeal or other review.

Usually the chairman of the board will open the interview by reviewing the highlights of your education and work experience from your application – primarily for the benefit of the other members of the board, as well as to get the material into the record. Do not interrupt or comment unless there is an error or significant misinterpretation; if that is the case, do not hesitate. But do not quibble about insignificant matters. Also, he will usually ask you some question about your education, experience or your present job – partly to get you to start talking and to establish the interviewing "rapport." He may start the actual questioning, or turn it over to one of the other members. Frequently, each member undertakes the questioning on a particular area, one in which he is perhaps most competent, so you can expect each member to participate in the examination. Because time is limited, you may also expect some rather abrupt switches in the direction the questioning takes, so do not be upset by it. Normally, a board member will not pursue a single line of questioning unless he discovers a particular strength or weakness.

After each member has participated, the chairman will usually ask whether any member has any further questions, then will ask you if you have anything you wish to add. Unless you are expecting this question, it may floor you. Worse, it may start you off on an extended, extemporaneous speech. The board is not usually seeking more information. The question is principally to offer you a last opportunity to present further qualifications or to indicate that you have nothing to add. So, if you feel that a significant qualification or characteristic has been overlooked, it is proper to point it out in a sentence or so. Do not compliment the board on the thoroughness of their examination – they have been sketchy, and you know it. If you wish, merely say, "No thank you, I have nothing further to add." This is a point where you can "talk yourself out" of a good impression or fail to present an important bit of information. Remember, *you close the interview yourself.*

The chairman will then say, "That is all, Mr. _____, thank you." Do not be startled; the interview is over, and quicker than you think. Thank him, gather your belongings and take your leave. Save your sigh of relief for the other side of the door.

How to put your best foot forward

Throughout this entire process, you may feel that the board individually and collectively is trying to pierce your defenses, seek out your hidden weaknesses and embarrass and confuse you. Actually, this is not true. They are obliged to make an appraisal of your qualifications for the job you are seeking, and they want to see you in your best light. Remember, they must interview all candidates and a non-cooperative candidate may become a failure in spite of their best efforts to bring out his qualifications. Here are 15 suggestions that will help you:

1) Be natural – Keep your attitude confident, not cocky

If you are not confident that you can do the job, do not expect the board to be. Do not apologize for your weaknesses, try to bring out your strong points. The board is interested in a positive, not negative, presentation. Cockiness will antagonize any board member and make him wonder if you are covering up a weakness by a false show of strength.

2) Get comfortable, but don't lounge or sprawl

Sit erectly but not stiffly. A careless posture may lead the board to conclude that you are careless in other things, or at least that you are not impressed by the importance of the occasion. Either conclusion is natural, even if incorrect. Do not fuss with your clothing, a pencil or an ashtray. Your hands may occasionally be useful to emphasize a point; do not let them become a point of distraction.

3) Do not wisecrack or make small talk

This is a serious situation, and your attitude should show that you consider it as such. Further, the time of the board is limited – they do not want to waste it, and neither should you.

4) Do not exaggerate your experience or abilities

In the first place, from information in the application or other interviews and sources, the board may know more about you than you think. Secondly, you probably will not get away with it. An experienced board is rather adept at spotting such a situation, so do not take the chance.

5) If you know a board member, do not make a point of it, yet do not hide it

Certainly you are not fooling him, and probably not the other members of the board. Do not try to take advantage of your acquaintanceship – it will probably do you little good.

6) Do not dominate the interview

Let the board do that. They will give you the clues – do not assume that you have to do all the talking. Realize that the board has a number of questions to ask you, and do not try to take up all the interview time by showing off your extensive knowledge of the answer to the first one.

7) Be attentive

You only have 20 minutes or so, and you should keep your attention at its sharpest throughout. When a member is addressing a problem or question to you, give him your undivided attention. Address your reply principally to him, but do not exclude the other board members.

8) Do not interrupt

A board member may be stating a problem for you to analyze. He will ask you a question when the time comes. Let him state the problem, and wait for the question.

9) Make sure you understand the question

Do not try to answer until you are sure what the question is. If it is not clear, restate it in your own words or ask the board member to clarify it for you. However, do not haggle about minor elements.

10) Reply promptly but not hastily

A common entry on oral board rating sheets is "candidate responded readily," or "candidate hesitated in replies." Respond as promptly and quickly as you can, but do not jump to a hasty, ill-considered answer.

11) Do not be peremptory in your answers

A brief answer is proper – but do not fire your answer back. That is a losing game from your point of view. The board member can probably ask questions much faster than you can answer them.

12) Do not try to create the answer you think the board member wants

He is interested in what kind of mind you have and how it works – not in playing games. Furthermore, he can usually spot this practice and will actually grade you down on it.

13) Do not switch sides in your reply merely to agree with a board member

Frequently, a member will take a contrary position merely to draw you out and to see if you are willing and able to defend your point of view. Do not start a debate, yet do not surrender a good position. If a position is worth taking, it is worth defending.

14) Do not be afraid to admit an error in judgment if you are shown to be wrong

The board knows that you are forced to reply without any opportunity for careful consideration. Your answer may be demonstrably wrong. If so, admit it and get on with the interview.

15) Do not dwell at length on your present job

The opening question may relate to your present assignment. Answer the question but do not go into an extended discussion. You are being examined for a *new* job, not your present one. As a matter of fact, try to phrase ALL your answers in terms of the job for which you are being examined.

Basis of Rating

Probably you will forget most of these "do's" and "don'ts" when you walk into the oral interview room. Even remembering them all will not ensure you a passing grade. Perhaps you did not have the qualifications in the first place. But remembering them will help you to put your best foot forward, without treading on the toes of the board members.

Rumor and popular opinion to the contrary notwithstanding, an oral board wants you to make the best appearance possible. They know you are under pressure – but they also want to see how you respond to it as a guide to what your reaction would be under the pressures of the job you seek. They will be influenced by the degree of poise you display, the personal traits you show and the manner in which you respond.

ABOUT THIS BOOK

This book contains tests divided into Examination Sections. Go through each test, answering every question in the margin. We have also attached a sample answer sheet at the back of the book that can be removed and used. At the end of each test look at the answer key and check your answers. On the ones you got wrong, look at the right answer choice and learn. Do not fill in the answers first. Do not memorize the questions and answers, but understand the answer and principles involved. On your test, the questions will likely be different from the samples. Questions are changed and new ones added. If you understand these past questions you should have success with any changes that arise. Tests may consist of several types of questions. We have additional books on each subject should more study be advisable or necessary for you. Finally, the more you study, the better prepared you will be. This book is intended to be the last thing you study before you walk into the examination room. Prior study of relevant texts is also recommended. NLC publishes some of these in our Fundamental Series. Knowledge and good sense are important factors in passing your exam. Good luck also helps. So now study this Passbook, absorb the material contained within and take that knowledge into the examination. Then do your best to pass that exam.

EXAMINATION SECTION

EXAMINATION SECTION
TEST 1

DIRECTIONS: Each question or incomplete statement is followed by several suggested answers or completions. Select the one that BEST answers the question or completes the statement. *PRINT THE LETTER OF THE CORRECT ANSWER IN THE SPACE AT THE RIGHT.*

1. A coagulase reaction is considered positive ONLY when

    A. the entire contents of the tube coagulates
    B. the entire clot turns black
    C. there is any degree of clotting
    D. a clot forms within 20 seconds

2. Salmonellae are MAINLY spread, directly or indirectly, by

    A. under-heated foods
    B. fecal contamination
    C. animal parasites
    D. an optimum pH of the water supply

3. The dilution water used for standard plate counts must be ONLY ____water.

    A. sterile tap
    B. sterile distilled
    C. phosphate buffered refined
    D. phosphate buffered tap

4. A medium used in plating should be melted and then held in a water bath until used at a temperature range BETWEEN

    A. 32-35° C
    B. 37-40° C
    C. 42-44° C
    D. 44-46° C

5. Thermoduric bacteria are defined as bacteria which

    A. produce heat
    B. cannot be destroyed by heat
    C. depend upon high temperatures to elaborate the BQC through the cell wall
    D. survive exposure to temperatures above their maximal temperatures for growth

6. Thermophilic bacteria are defined as bacteria which

    A. cannot endure heat
    B. have an optimum growth temperature below 50° C
    C. have an optimum growth temperature above 50° C
    D. absorb heat

7. Of the following pairs of tests and results, the one which exhibits TWO of the characteristics of salmonella is

A. urease negative and phenol red dulcitol positive
B. lysine decarboxylase negative and KCN negative
C. malonate positive and indole negative
D. polyvalent flagellar positive, polyvalent somatic negative

8. Petri dishes should NOT be sterilized and stored in containers made of

   A. aluminum
   B. copper
   C. stainless steel
   D. borisilicate glass

9. Of the following temperatures, the one which is the PROPER incubation for the standard plate count on water using an agar medium for 24 hours 2 hours is

   A. $20° \pm 0.5°C$
   B. $32° \pm 0.5°C$
   C. $35° \pm 0..5°C$
   D. $37° \pm 0.5°C$

10. The one of the following which can be identified by a test in which the production of gas from lactose in suitable culture medium at $44.5°C \pm 0.5°C$ can be used is the

    A. thiobacilli
    B. pseudomonas
    C. fecal section of the coliform group
    D. acetobacter

11. Which one of the following groups of tests comprise the IMVIC? Indole,

    A. Methyl red, Voges-proskauer, and Sodium citrate
    B. Methylene blue, Voges-proskauer, and Kovae's reagent
    C. Methyl red, Voges-proskauer, and Citric acid
    D. Phenol red, Voges-proskauer, and Sodium citrate

12. In filling a water sample bottle, the CORRECT method is to fill it

    A. with a siphon
    B. to the stopper to prevent air from entering
    C. by removing the stopper and hood as a unit with care to eliminate soiling
    D. by removing the stopper and hood, and waiting two minutes for the water to clear the line

13. A bacterial mutant blocked in a biosynthetic step is called

    A. auxotrophic
    B. prototrophic
    C. transformed
    D. transduced

14. Bacterial DNA is NOT associated with

    A. putrescine
    B. histone
    C. spermine
    D. cadaverine

15. When using light microscopy, which one of the following staining, procedures can be used to detect bacterial DNA?

    A. Sudan B. Black
    B. Lactophenol cotton blue
    C. Fuelgen
    D. Ziehl-Neelsen

16. Protoplasts can be obtained from gram positive cells by treatment with lysozme, provided that the solution in which they are suspended is

    A. hypertonic
    B. hypotonic
    C. isotonic
    D. non-ionic

17. In cells capable of metabolizing glucose both aerobically and anaerobically, the sugar will disappear more rapidly under anaerobic than under aerobic conditions.
    This inhibition of glycolysis, first recognized in fermenting yeast, is known as the

    A. Guerbet Reaction
    B. Pasteur Effect
    C. Fries Rule
    D. Gallagher-Hollander Degradation

18. Bacteria do NOT produce intracellular organelle(s) such as

    A. a murine sacculus
    B. mesosomes
    C. inclusion bodies
    D. mitochondria

19. The production of pili can be tested for by flooding bacterial colonies on the surface of an agar plate with

    A. Kovac's reagent
    B. 1% solution of tetramethyl-p-phenylenediamine
    C. 10% sodium deoxycholate followed by methenamine silver nitrate solution
    D. concentrated suspension of R.B.C. and rinsing with saline

20. Vibrio comma is a member of the family

    A. Pseudomonadaceae
    B. Spriellaceae
    C. Enterobacteriaceae
    D. Brusellaceae

21. Bacteria that produce food spoilage at 5° C (41° F) are termed

    A. anthrotrophic
    B. mesophilic
    C. psychrotrophic
    D. thermophilic

22. Bacillus stearothermophilus is an organism which

    A. causes gas gangrene
    B. is primarily used in fermentation of sausage blends
    C. causes morbilliform eruptions
    D. is used to check the proper function of the autoclave

23. Balamuths medium is used in the cultivation of

    A. Brucella abortus
    B. Mycobacterium tuberculosis
    C. Candida albicans
    D. Entamoeba histolytica

24. Of the following processes, the one in which PVA (poly-vinyl alcohol) is used is

A. the examination of material for mycoplasma
B. digesting sputum in the T.B. laboratory
C. the Giemsa Stain method
D. fixation of trophozoites in stools

25. In examining fecal film preparations, protozoan cysts can READILY be distinguished by the use of ____ solution.

   A. Rees
   B. Weinmans Barium
   C. Tables
   D. Dobell and O'Conners Iodine

26. The purpose of a candle jar used in the incubation of a culture is to supply a source of

   A. nitrous oxide
   B. oxygen
   C. hydrogen
   D. carbon dioxide

27. Of the following, the gauge of the syringe needle having the SMALLEST diameter is

   A. 18
   B. 19
   C. 22
   D. 26

28. The percentage of phenol in a disinfecting solution is

   A. 1%
   B. 5%
   C. 10%
   D. 50%

29. The niacin test is considered positive if the ALMOST IMMEDIATE reaction results in the production of

   A. a green color
   B. a black metallic precipitate
   C. a yellow color
   D. 50 mm of bubbles

30. One use of optochin disks (ethyl hydrocupreine HCL) is

   A. to supply the V factor
   B. in the oxidase test
   C. to distinguish Brucella species
   D. to differentiate between Pneumococci and alpha hemolytic streptococci

31. Media suggested for the isolation of Vibrio comma from fecal specimens have a pH of

   A. 8.5
   B. 5.0
   C. 7.0
   D. 13.0

32. A method of NO value in the grouping of Shigella is

   A. testing of fimbral antigens
   B. K antigens
   C. Colicin typing
   D. flagella antigens

33. A biochemical test or substrate MOST useful in differentiating between the genus Providencia and the genus Shigella is

   A. glucose
   B. urease
   C. Arginine dihydrolase
   D. phenylalanine deaminase

34. A medium of choice USEFUL in the selective isolation of Pseudomonas aeruginosa is _____ agar.

    A. Bismuth Sulfite
    B. Cystine Tellurite
    C. Fletchers
    D. Agaricus

35. The antigenetic formula *055:B5* is a sera type of

    A. Salmonella
    B. Shigella
    C. Escherichia
    D. Enterobacter

36. The BEST way to distinguish the genus Proteus from other members of the Enterobacteriaceae is that they

    A. are oxidose positive
    B. utilize urea rapidly
    C. produce a green pigment
    D. are phenylalanine deaminase negative

37. In identifying Salmonella, the term *diphasic* infers that

    A. the phase may or may not be motile
    B. phases have the same *O* antigens but different *H* antigens
    C. phases have the same *E* antigens but different *O* antigens
    D. the *Vi* antigen may or may not be present

38. When inoculated into TSI slants, typical Shigella form an

    A. alkaline slant no gas in butt H_2S^-
    B. alkaline slant gas in butt H_2S^+
    C. acid slant gas in butt H_2S^-
    D. acid slant gas in butt H_2S^+

39. Ken broth is a medium useful in distinguishing members of the family

    A. Neisseriaceae
    B. Streptococceae
    C. Brucellaceae
    D. Enterbacteriaceae

40. Two characteristics of the bacteria of the genus Klebsiella are that they are

    A. non-motile and liquify sodium pectate
    B. non-motile and encapsulated
    C. motile and oxidize glucose
    D. motile rods (gram+) that exhibit pleomorphism

41. In serological identification of gram-negative enteric bacteria, the term *H* antigens refers to _____ antigens.

    A. capsular   B. somatic   C. pilin   D. flagella

42. The coagulase tube test is used in the identification of which one of the following?

    A. Corynebacteria
    B. Gram-negative rods
    C. Gram-positive cocci
    D. Pathogenic yeasts

43. A medium of choice in the isolation of N. gonorrhoeae is
    A. Bismuth Sulfite Agar
    B. Bordet - Gerigou
    C. Forget - Fredette Agar
    D. Thayer - Martin Agar

44. Streptococcus fecalis, when classified by the Lancefield system, is placed in Group
    A. A
    B. B
    C. C
    D. D

45. The biochemical inulin is classified as a(n)
    A. carbohydrate
    B. amino acid
    C. fatty acid
    D. tricarboxylic acid

KEY (CORRECT ANSWERS)

1. C	11. A	21. C	31. A	41. D
2. B	12. C	22. D	32. D	42. C
3. B	13. A	23. D	33. D	43. D
4. D	14. B	24. D	34. A	44. D
5. D	15. C	25. D	35. C	45. A
6. C	16. A	26. D	36. B	
7. A	17. B	27. D	37. B	
8. B	18. D	28. B	38. A	
9. C	19. D	29. C	39. D	
10. C	20. B	30. D	40. B	

TEST 2

DIRECTIONS: Each question or incomplete statement is followed by several suggested answers or completions. Select the one that BEST answers the question or completes the statement. *PRINT THE LETTER OF THE CORRECT ANSWER IN THE SPACE AT THE RIGHT.*

1. Of the fermentation patterns shown, the one which is exhibited by a typical strain of Neisseria gonorrhoeae is   1.____

    A. glucose + maltose + sucrose -
    B. glucose + maltose - sucrose -
    C. glucose - maltose - sucrose -
    D. glucose + maltose + sucrose +

2. A characteristic of Staphylococci which distinguishes it from Streptococci is that Staphylococci are   2.____

    A. catalase positive and reduce nitrates to nitrites
    B. oxidase positive
    C. bile soluble
    D. obligate anaerobes

3. The one of the following which BEST describes the method or procedure of inspissation is   3.____

    A. the removal of tissue for biopsy
    B. the separation of protein fractions of body fluids
    C. serologic analysis
    D. preparation of various bacteriological media sensitive to high temperatures

4. The intestinal protozoan Balantidium coli is classified as a(n)   4.____

    A. ciliate   B. flagellate   C. ameba   D. sporozoan

5. Scotochromogens are mycobacteria that   5.____

    A. can form pigments in the dark
    B. form pigments in the light only
    C. are saprophytic members of Ruyon Group IV
    D. rapidly reduce tellurite

6. A bacterial culture described as phage type 80/81 refers to a strain of   6.____

    A. Neisseria meningitidis
    B. Coynebacterium diphtheriae
    C. Staphylococcus aureus
    D. Salmonella enteritidis

7. Tsutsugamushi disease is caused by a member of the   7.____

    A. Chlamydiaceae   B. Rickettsiaceae
    C. Bacillaceae   D. Spirochaetaceae

8. Pinworm infection is caused by the organism   8.____

A. Trichinella spiralis
B. Nicator Americanus
C. Ascaris lumbricoides
D. Enterobius vermicularis

9. Nocardia species differ from Actinomyces in that Nocardia are

   A. obligate parasites
   B. not acid fast
   C. anaerobic
   D. partially acid fast aerobic faculative parasites

10. The family Actinomycetaceae includes species of Actinomyces and Nocardia. These organisms are identified as

    A. gram-positive cocci
    B. gram-negative cocci
    C. gram-positive branching organisms
    D. yeast-like organisms

11. Coccidioidomycosis is an infectious disease caused by Coccidioides immitis. Which of the following ways BEST explains how man acquires this disease? By

    A. coming into contact with an infected human
    B. eating food contaminated by Rattus brevicaudatus
    C. being bitten by an infected flea
    D. developing a dust-borne respiratory infection

12. In direct microscopic examination of sputum gastric washings, excudates or pus, C. immitis appears

    A. as a large budding encapsulated yeast
    B. as a non-budding, thick-walled spherule, containing numerous small endospores
    C. intracellularly as small round or oval yeast-like cells
    D. as tuberculate macroconidia

13. In the laboratory, M. fortuitum is identified by

    A. its ability to produce pigment in the light
    B. a positive three-day aryl sulfatase test and growth on MacConkey agar
    C. a strongly positive Niacin test
    D. its inability to grow on artificial media

14. Erythrogenic toxin is known to be the cause for the rash in scarlet fever. The organism producing this toxin is

    A. Group III pneumococcus
    B. Group A streptococcus
    C. Staphylococcus aureus
    D. Corynebacterium haemolyticum

15. One reason penicillin is an effective antibiotic is that it

    A. interferes with cell wall synthesis and lyses growing cells
    B. interacts with ribosomes

C. inhibits utilization of Para amino benzoate
D. inhibits DNA synthesis but not RNA and protein synthesis

16. Treponema pallidium is the causative treponeme of syphilis. Cultivation of pathogenic treponema

    A. is accomplished by Acetate Medium
    B. is accomplished by Albizo-Surgalla Serum Agar
    C. is accomplished by Balamuth Egg Infusion Medium
    D. has not been accomplished in vitro

17. Characteristic strains of Pseudomonos aerugenosa isolated from sputum of cystic fibrosis patients are BEST described as

    A. non-mucin producing
    B. mucin producing
    C. R-types
    D. oxidase negative

18. Strains of Klebsiella can be distinguished from those of Enterobacter by the use of ____ agar.

    A. MacConkey   B. Motility   C. EMB   D. TSI

19. Staphylococcus aureus elaborates a variety of metabolites. The metabolite commonly found to be the cause of food poisoning is

    A. hemolysin
    B. enterotoxin
    C. leukocidin
    D. phosphatase

20. A biochemical test that is used to differentiate between Providencia and Proteus is

    A. methyl red
    B. malonate utilization
    C. raffinose fermentation
    D. urease

21. The one of the following which are the typical coli biochemical reactions is:

    A. Indole -, methyl red -, voges proskauer +, citrate +
    B. Indole +, methyl red +, voges proskauer -, citrate -
    C. Indole -, methyl red +, voges proskauer -, citrate +
    D. Indole +, methyl red +, voges proskauer -, citrate +

22. The optimum pH for salmonella growth is

    A. 8.6 0.2
    B. 7.6 0.2
    C. 6.8 0.2
    D. 6.0 0.2

23. The color of typical salmonella colonies on bismuth sulfite agar appears

    A. colorless, pink to fuchsia
    B. yellow-green or green
    C. brown, gray to black
    D. medium orange to red

24. A molar solution contains one gram____ml of solution.

    A. equivalent weight of solute per 1000
    B. molecular weight of solute per 1000

C. equivalent weight of solute per 100
D. molecular weight of solute per 100

25. The symbol *1+9 HCl* denotes that

    A. 1 volume of concentrated HCl is to be diluted with 9 volumes of distilled water
    B. 1 normal HCl is added to 9 normal HCl
    C. 9 volumes of concentrated HCl is diluted with 1 volume of water
    D. 1 molal HCl is diluted with 9 volumes of distilled water

26. In the somatic cell counting of stained films, the cells which should be counted include

    A. each somatic cell with an identifiable stained nucleus
    B. any fragment of a cell
    C. only those cells measuring 300 microns
    D. only those cells measuring 600 microns

27. Petri dishes placed into an incubator for the standard plate count MUST reach the temperature of incubation within a time period of _____ hour(s).

    A. 1/2   B. 1   C. 1 1/2   D. 2

28. The microbial density of air (bacteria, yeasts, and molds) in plating areas should NOT exceed_____ colonies/plate during_____minute exposure.

    A. 5; 10   B. 10; 15   C. 15; 15   D. 20; 25

29. In order for a pH meter to stabilize, the amount of time it optimumly should be turned on before use is_____ minutes.

    A. 5   B. 10   C. 30   D. 60

30. The membrane filter technique is an effective method for the detection of

    A. pollution in water   B. viral infections
    C. infectious hepatitis   D. radionuclides

31. The time elapsing between collection and examination of water for bacteriologic examination should NOT exceed _____ hours.

    A. 10   B. 20   C. 30   D. 40

32. A substance which should be used to dechlorinate a water sample containing residual chlorine is

    A. boric acid   B. HTH
    C. Sodium thiosulfate   D. Quaternary compound

33. The reason for examining non-potable water is GENERALLY to

    A. estimate the density of bacterial contamination
    B. check the level of chloramines
    C. determine the treatment necessary
    D. determine the presence of salmonella

34. Swabs made of calcium aliginate fibers are soluble in aqueous solutions containing   34.____

    A. 1% of sodium hexametaphosphate
    B. 1% of sodium carbonate
    C. 2% of aluminum oxide
    D. 1% of ferric oxide

35. What percent of NaCl should tripticase soy broth contain when testing for coagulase positive staphyloeocci?   35.____

    A. 2%   B. -5%   C. 7%   D. 10%

36. In blood grouping, the *H* antigen is found PRIMARILY in the genotype   36.____

    A. AB   B. AA   C. BB   D. OO

37. The Weil-Felix test depends on rickettsial antiserum cross-reacting with strains of   37.____

    A. Proteus   B. Escherichia
    C. Salmonella   D. Enterobacter

38. In gram stain preparations of blood or smears from tissues of living animals infected with Bacillus anthracis, the organism appears in the form of a   38.____

    A. gram+ sporeforming rod
    B. gram- sporeforming rod
    C. gram+ non-sporeformed encapsulated rod
    D. gram+ rod exhibiting Babes-Ernst bodies

39. Shigella are classified in subgroups.
    Subgroup A is characterized by its inability to ferment   39.____

    A. Lactose   B. Sucrose   C. Mannitol   D. Xylose

40. In grouping Shigella organisms identified as Sh. sonnei would be placed in Group   40.____

    A. A   B. B   C. C   D. D

41. Streptococcus pyogenes, when grouped by the Lancefield method, is in Group   41.____

    A. A   B. E   C. L   D. N

42. Of the intestinal ameba found in man, the organism thought NOT to have a cyst stage is   42.____

    A. Entamoeba histolytica   B. Entamoeba coli
    C. Endolimax nana   D. Dientamoeba fragilis

43. Melioidosis is a disease found in U.S. troops in Vietnam. The causative agent is   43.____

    A. Pasturella multocidia
    B. Pseudomonas pseudomallei
    C. Bordetella bronchiseptica
    D. Brucella melitensis

44. The so-called *universal recipient* is blood group   44.____

    A. AO   B. BO   C. AB   D. OO

45. In blood grouping, the term amorph would be requested by the allelic diploid 45.____
 A. AB B. AA C. AO D. OO

KEY (CORRECT ANSWERS)

1. B	11. D	21. B	31. C	41. A
2. A	12. B	22. C	32. C	42. D
3. D	13. B	23. C	33. A	43. B
4. A	14. B	24. B	34. A	44. C
5. A	15. A	25. A	35. D	45. A
6. C	16. D	26. A	36. D	
7. B	17. B	27. D	37. A	
8. D	18. B	28. C	38. C	
9. D	19. B	29. C	39. C	
10. C	20. D	30. A	40. D	

EXAMINATION SECTION
TEST 1

DIRECTIONS: Each question or incomplete statement is followed by several suggested answers or completions. Select the one that BEST answers the question or completes the statement. *PRINT THE LETTER OF THE CORRECT ANSWER IN THE SPACE AT THE RIGHT.*

1. Of the following, the one which is LEAST satisfactory as a differential coliform test is 1.____

    A. citrate utilization
    B. gelatin liquefaction
    C. methyl-red
    D. Voges-Proskauer

2. The cholera vibrio is 2.____

    A. atrichous
    B. amphitrichous
    C. monotrichous
    D. perltrichous

3. The tetanus bacilli are classified as 3.____

    A. aerobes
    B. facultative anaerobes
    C. micro-aerophiles
    D. obligate anaerobes

4. Milk is pasteurized in order to destroy all 4.____

    A. bacteria
    B. non-spore forming bacteria
    C. non-spore forming pathogens
    D. spore forming pathogens

5. The IMVIC for typical strains of E.coli is 5.____

    A. + + + +   B. + + − −   C. − − + +   D. − − − −

6. The term *peritrichous* means having 6.____

    A. a single flagellum at one pole
    B. a tuft of flagella at one pole
    C. flagella at both poles
    D. flagella completely surrounding the body

7. Bacteria belonging to the genus Thiothrix are GENERALLY called _____ bacteria. 7.____

    A. iron
    B. nitrifying
    C. sulfate-reducing
    D. sulfur

8. Bacteria belonging to the genus Crenothrix are GENERALLY termed _____ bacteria. 8.____

    A. iron
    B. nitrifying
    C. sulfate-reducing
    D. sulfur

9. The one of the following which is NOT characteristic of the coliform group is 9.____

    A. ferment lactose
    B. Gram-negative
    C. non-gas former
    D. non-spore former

10. The organism, Aerobacter aerogenes, is USUALLY considered to be a(n) _____ coliform organism.

   A. fecal
   B. intestinal
   C. non-fecal
   D. pathogenic

11. The term *plankton* includes all organisms that are microscopic or barely visible to the naked eye, with the exception of the

   A. bacteria   B. Crustacea   C. protozoa   D. rotifera

12. The one of the following methods GENERALLY associated with the concentration of water samples for water analysis is the _____ method.

   A. Kjeldahl
   B. Sedgwick-Rafter
   C. Winkler
   D. Zeolite

13. The ortho-tolidine method is GENERALLY used to measure

   A. copper
   B. nitrite nitrogen
   C. orthophosphate
   D. residual chlorine

14. A study of water-borne epidemics in the United States reveals that the disease responsible for the GREATEST number of cases is

   A. anthrax
   B. Asiatic cholera
   C. dysentery
   D. tuberculosis

15. The name of the organism causing non-bacillary dysentery is

   A. Endameba coli
   B. Endameba histolytica
   C. Escherichia coli
   D. Shigella sonnei

16. The immunity acquired against tuberculosis by prophylactic vaccination with BCG is _____ acquired _____ immunity.

   A. artificially; active
   B. artificially; passive
   C. naturally; active
   D. naturally; passive

17. The optimum temperature of growth for MOST pathogenic bacteria is APPROXIMATELY

   A. 20° C   B. 20° F   C. 37° C   D. 37° F

18. Of the following diseases, the one NOT caused by an acid-fast organism is

   A. Johne's disease
   B. leprosy
   C. pertussis
   D. tuberculosis

19. The presence of Vi antibodies in the human serum is indicative of an infection of

   A. cholera
   B. salmonellosis
   C. shigellosis
   D. typhoid fever

20. The causative agents of salmonellosis are gram-_____, lactose _____ rods.

   A. negative; negative
   B. negative; positive
   C. positive; negative
   D. positive; positive

21. Of the following, the organism MOST resistant to disinfecting agents is the one causing 21._____

   A. amebic dysentery B. bacillary dysentery
   C. cholera D. typhoid

22. The FIRST step in the recommended procedure for cleaning glassware containing infectious material is 22._____

   A. rinsing B. scraping
   C. sterilizing D. washing

23. The MOST heat-resistant of the pathogens *generally* found in milk is 23._____

   A. Salmonella typhosa B. Mycobacterium tuberculosis
   C. Shigella sonnei D. Streptococcus pyogenes

24. The hydrogen-ion concentration of culture media increases during sterilization. The USUAL decrease in the pH reading as a result of sterilization is *approximately* 24._____

   A. 0.3   B. 0.8   C. 1.4   D. 2.7

25. The PRINCIPAL ingredients of nutrient broth are 25._____

   A. beef extract and peptone
   B. beef extract and glucose
   C. ground beef and peptone
   D. ground beef and glucose

KEY (CORRECT ANSWERS)

1. B		11. A	
2. C		12. B	
3. D		13. D	
4. C		14. C	
5. B		15. B	
6. D		16. A	
7. D		17. C	
8. A		18. C	
9. C		19. D	
10. C		20. A	

21. A
22. C
23. B
24. A
25. A

TEST 2

DIRECTIONS: Each question or incomplete statement is followed by several suggested answers or completions. Select the one that BEST answers the question or completes the statement. *PRINT THE LETTER OF THE CORRECT ANSWER IN THE SPACE AT THE RIGHT.*

1. The solidifying point of agar is APPROXIMATELY 1.____
   A. 25° C B. 40° C C. 55° C D. 70° C

2. The one of the following NOT contained in Krumwiede Triple Sugar Agar is 2.____
   A. dextrose B. lactose C. maltose D. sucrose

3. The indicator GENERALLY used in Krumwiede Triple Sugar Agar is 3.____
   A. bromcresol purple
   B. litmus
   C. methyl orange
   D. phenol red

4. The one of the following which is NOT an ingredient of Endo medium is 4.____
   A. agar
   B. basic fuchsin
   C. glucose
   D. lactose

5. Endo medium when cooled is 5.____
   A. blue B. colorless C. green D. yellow

6. The color of the colonies produced by Escherichia coli on Endo medium is 6.____
   A. blue B. brown C. green D. red

7. The gas produced in the fermentation of lactose is ESSENTIALLY 7.____
   A. CO B. CO_2 C. H_2 D. H_2O

8. The Barrett method is GENERALLY used to determine production of 8.____
   A. acetyl-methyl-carbinol
   B. hydrogen sulfide
   C. indol
   D. urea

9. The color of the test reagent in a positive indol test is 9.____
   A. dark blue
   B. dark red
   C. light green
   D. light yellow

10. Indol is a decomposition product of 10.____
    A. amyl alcohol
    B. lactose
    C. paradimethylaminobenzaldehyde
    D. tryptophane

11. A sodium citrate positive test is indicated if, after 96 hours of incubation, there is 11.____
    A. a red color
    B. a yellow color
    C. no growth
    D. visible growth

12. A positive Voges-Proskauer test is GENERALLY indicated by the appearance of a _____ color.

    A. blue   B. green   C. red   D. yellow

13. Phosphate is added to the test medium used for the methyl red test to provide a(n)

    A. buffer
    B. food supply
    C. indicator
    D. inhibitor

14. The Kjeldahl method is used to analyze for

    A. chlorine   B. copper   C. iron   D. nitrogen

15. Amino acids are formed in the hydrolysis of

    A. disaccharides
    B. fats
    C. monosaccharides
    D. proteins

16. The one of the following that is NOT classified as a disaccharide is

    A. glucose   B. lactose   C. maltose   D. sucrose

17. The process of culturing bacteria by providing them with the necessary conditions for growth is known as

    A. incubation
    B. inoculation
    C. sterilization
    D. staining

18. Blood typing is necessary in the transfusion of

    A. amino acids
    B. dextrose
    C. plasma
    D. whole blood

19. The BEST method of preventing the spread of the common cold is to treat the patient by

    A. injecting antitoxin
    B. isolating him
    C. administering sulfa drugs
    D. vaccinating him

20. Requiring food handlers to undergo a periodic health examination might reduce the number of cases of

    A. scurvy
    B. tetanus
    C. typhoid fever
    D. yellow fever

21. Jumping at a sudden noise is an example of a

    A. habit
    B. simple reflex
    C. conditioned reflex
    D. voluntary act

22. Which vitamin is MOST easily destroyed by heat or air?

    A. A   B. B   C. C   D. D

23. Which is a product of fermentation by yeasts?

    A. Alcohol   B. Oxygen   C. Nitrogen   D. Starch

24. A drop of milk was placed on each of several culture medium preparations and then incubated for several days. No bacterial colonies developed.
    The milk MOST probably had been

    A. boiled
    B. pasteurized
    C. refrigerated
    D. skimmed

25. MOST antibodies have been isolated from organisms that live in

    A. water B. air C. soil D. animals

KEY (CORRECT ANSWERS)

1. B		11. D	
2. C		12. C	
3. D		13. A	
4. C		14. D	
5. B		15. D	
6. D		16. A	
7. B		17. A	
8. A		18. D	
9. B		19. B	
10. D		20. C	

21. A
22. C
23. A
24. A
25. C

EXAMINATION SECTION
TEST 1

DIRECTIONS: Each question or incomplete statement is followed by several suggested answers or completions. Select the one that BEST answers the question or completes the statement. *PRINT THE LETTER OF THE CORRECT ANSWER IN THE SPACE AT THE RIGHT.*

1. According to Department regulations, whenever meat is packaged by a retailer in advance of being sold, which one of the following MUST also be provided not more than 30 feet from the display counter? 1.____

    A. A chart indicating the date the item must be removed from sale
    B. A chart indicating the date the item was first placed on sale
    C. A means of testing the item for adulteration
    D. An accurate computing scale marked "for customer use" or a sign telling customers where such scale is located

2. According to Department regulations, retail stores are NOT permitted to sell prepackaged meat unless the package is 2.____

    A. colorless and transparent
    B. less than one ounce in weight
    C. of a heat-resistant material
    D. open at one end

3. Hamburger meat may contain all of the following EXCEPT 3.____

    A. chemical preservatives   B. added fat
    C. chuck steak   D. neck meat

4. The net weight declaration on a package of food MUST be 4.____

    A. in grams as well as ounces
    B. near the top of the package
    C. on the label but in no specific place
    D. on the main panel of the label

5. The fat content of oleomargarine MUST be at least 5.____

    A. 40 percent   B. 60 percent
    C. 80 percent   D. 90 percent

6. The following foods contain standardized ingredients EXCEPT 6.____

    A. ice cream   B. jams and jellies
    C. ketchup   D. orange drink

7. Earthenware dishes very often affect food stored in them by being the source of 7.____

    A. asbestos contamination   B. bacteria
    C. lead contamination   D. fluid dyes

8. The presence of E. Coli in food PROBABLY means that it

   A. is contaminated by fecal matter
   B. is high in minerals
   C. is suitable for diabetics
   D. must be refrigerated

9. Botulism food poisoning in the United States is *usually* caused by

   A. eating fish caught in polluted waters
   B. failure to wash raw fruit before eating
   C. improper home-canning of fruits and vegetables
   D. tapeworms found in beef or sheep

10. Food poisoning cases in the United States are *usually* characterized by

    A. long periods of illness followed by death
    B. long periods of illness rarely followed by death
    C. short periods of illness followed by death
    D. short periods of illness rarely followed by death

11. In the United States, food poisoning due to eating mushrooms is LARGELY attributable to

    A. failure to cook mushrooms
    B. failure to wash mushrooms
    C. mushrooms which are blue in color
    D. mushrooms which have not been cultivated domestically

12. Decomposition of fresh or cold storage meats can be detected BEST by

    A. noting absence of surface moisture
    B. noting presence of "off" odors
    C. noting warmth when touched
    D. observing discoloration

13. Bacterial control of shellfish and shellfish growing areas is being based increasingly in this country upon the density of the Escherichia coli organisms in the waters from which shellfish are collected.
    The BEST reason for this is that

    A. E. coli are virulent pathogens which produce serious diseases in man
    B. the density of E. coli in water is relatively easy to determine by shellfish fishermen
    C. the presence of E. coli is an indicator of the presence of human wastes in the water
    D. shellfish which ingest E. coli have objectionable odors which canning cannot remove

14. Proper cleaning of dairy utensils entails rinsing with

    A. cold or lukewarm water followed by scrubbing with a detergent solution
    B. cold or lukewarm water followed by scrubbing with hot soapy water
    C. hot water followed by scrubbing with a detergent solution
    D. hot water followed by scrubbing with hot soapy water

3 (#1)

15. Of the following foods, the type that is *most likely* to cause "staph" food poisoning if improperly prepared or handled is   15.____

    A. sugar-coated food   B. dried food
    C. pickled food   D. cream-filled food

16. Harmful bacteria are *most often* introduced into foods prepared in a food service operation by   16.____

    A. insects   B. rodents
    C. employees   D. utensils

17. The one of the following procedures that could cause food poisoning is   17.____

    A. allowing cooked poultry to stand for an hour, slicing it and covering it with broth, and holding it at room temperature for several hours
    B. keeping food mixtures on cafeteria counters for one hour
    C. cooking left-over food mixtures quickly by frequent stirring and then refrigerating in shallow pans
    D. chilling all ingredients for salads at least one hour before preparation

18. Trichinosis is a disease which may be caused by   18.____

    A. eating ham which has been overcooked
    B. unsanitary handling of frozen meats
    C. eating food which has been contaminated by infected flies
    D. eating infected pork which has been cooked insufficiently

19. Of the following, the bacteria which causes MOST food poisoning cases is   19.____

    A. botulinum   B. salmonella
    C. pneumococci   D. streptococci

20. Of the following, the BEST reason for discarding the green part of potatoes is that it contains a poison known a   20.____

    A. cevitamic acid   B. citric acid
    C. solanine   D. trichinae

21. Of the following, the most effective way to prevent consumption of botulism bacteria is to   21.____

    A. buy food products from supermarkets only
    B. discard canned goods that are bulging or foul-smelling
    C. discard all produce that is not organic
    D. use stainless steel cookware to prepare meals

22. Trichinosis is a disease caused by   22.____

    A. a worm   B. an allergy
    C. improper refrigeration   D. food adulteration

23. The ONLY safe method of canning non-acid vegetables and meats is the   23.____

    A. open kettle   B. hot water bath
    C. pressure process   D. cold pack

24. Spoilage in canned foods which is caused by bacteria that produces acid without gas is known as

    A. putrefaction
    B. fermentation
    C. botulinus
    D. flat-sour spoilage

25. To avoid the development of bacterial toxins in custards and cream pies, one should

    A. cool to room temperature before refrigeration
    B. refrigerate within half hour after cooking
    C. heat to 212° F. during cooking
    D. store in the freezing compartment

26. An excellent medium for the growth of bacteria which cause food poisoning toxins is

    A. cream puffs
    B. pickled watermelon rind
    C. nougat candies
    D. preserves

27. Cooked foods should be cooled and refrigerated quickly PRIMARILY to

    A. prevent growth and development of bacteria
    B. preserve food nutrients
    C. prevent loss of moisture content
    D. preserve a fresh-cooked appearance

28. Aerobic bacteria which cause food spoilage

    A. are unable to grow without air
    B. are able to grow without air
    C. grow equally well with or without air
    D. need heat and moisture for growth

29. A disease caused by contamination in canned foods is

    A. trichinosis
    B. botulism
    C. undulant fever
    D. tularemia

30. Oysters which feed on sewage sometimes transmit

    A. rabies
    B. yellow fever
    C. typhoid fever
    D. malaria

31. In order to retard spoilage of bread, many baking companies add

    A. sodium sulphathionate
    B. sodium propionate
    C. sodium hypophosphate
    D. sodium benzoate

32. Spoilage in canned foods may be caused by

    A. filling the jars with food and fluid even with the top
    B. allowing the jars to cool before sealing the jars completely
    C. heating the jars for use in the hot-pack method
    D. filling the jars with the liquid in which the food was cooked

33. To prevent curdling of mayonnaise,   33.____

    A. expose to light
    B. expose to air
    C. store at 32° F.
    D. store at 150° F.

34. When a retailer plans to offer for sale thawed meat or fish, he is required by Department   34.____
    regulations to do which one of the following?

    A. Label the product "thawed" or "defrosted"
    B. Reduce the price of the product
    C. Refreeze the product and label it "refrozen"
    D. Remove the unsold portion from sale within three hours

35. Certain perishable foods must be stamped, printed, or otherwise plainly and conspicu-   35.____
    ously marked with either the last day or date of sale or the last day or date of recom-
    mended usage. Among these foods are

    A. bread, meat and poultry
    B. bread, milk and meat
    C. eggs, bread and milk
    D. eggs, milk and poultry

KEY (CORRECT ANSWERS)

1.	D	16.	C
2.	A	17.	A
3.	A	18.	D
4.	D	19.	B
5.	C	20.	C
6.	D	21.	B
7.	C	22.	A
8.	A	23.	C
9.	C	24.	D
10.	D	25.	B
11.	D	26.	A
12.	B	27.	A
13.	C	28.	A
14.	A	29.	B
15.	D	30.	C

31. B
32. B
33. A
34. C
35. C

TEST 2

DIRECTIONS: Each question or incomplete statement is followed by several suggested answers or completions. Select the one that BEST answers the question or completes the statement. *PRINT THE LETTER OF THE CORRECT ANSWER IN THE SPACE AT THE RIGHT.*

1. Trichinae are destroyed by   1.___

   A. freezing and storing at 15° F
   B. curing in a 2.5% salt solution
   C. radiation sterilization
   D. heating to 125° F

2. Dishes used by a patient with a communicable disease should be   2.___

   A. *boiled* for 5 minutes in soapy water
   B. *boiled* in an antiseptic solution
   C. *washed* for 5 minutes in soapy hot water
   D. *washed* in clear water at 180° F

3. The medium of infection which is MOST difficult to control is   3.___

   A. insects   B. food   C. water   D. air

4. Bread spoilage is retarded by the addition of   4.___

   A. sodium carbonate   B. calcium propionate
   C. tartaric acid   D. protease

5. Frozen foods which have partially thawed   5.___

   A. may be refrozen
   B. may be cooked and refrozen
   C. must be discarded
   D. may be refrozen only after complete thawing

6. Pasteurization of milk   6.___

   A. kills pathogenic bacteria
   B. retards the growth of bacteria
   C. kills all bacteria
   D. homogenizes

7. Among the following food additives, the one which is used for the purpose of enhancing the keeping quality of the food is   7.___

   A. vitamin D in milk
   B. bleaching agents in flour
   C. scorbic acid in cider
   D. minerals and vitamins in cereals

8. An example of the bactericidal method of food preservation is   8.___

   A. jam and jellies   B. pickling
   C. freezing   D. refrigeration

9. Oysters which feed on sewage sometimes transmit

   A. rabies
   B. yellow fever
   C. typhoid fever
   D. malaria

10. The ONLY edible mussel that is sold is the

    A. scampi
    B. scallop
    C. clam
    D. rock lobster

11. *Flat sour*

    A. is spoilage of canned food by bacteria with formation of gas
    B. renders food unfit for consumption
    C. can be corrected by addition of sugar to food before serving
    D. should be re-boiled before serving

12. Trichinosis is a disease caused by

    A. a worm
    B. an allergy
    C. improper refrigeration
    D. food adulteration

13. Dry foods should be stored in

    A. a cool dry place
    B. the basement
    C. a cabinet near the stove
    D. the refrigerator

14. In the process of food preservation,

    A. all bacteria are destroyed
    B. harmful bacteria are destroyed
    C. the growth of bacteria may be prevented or checked
    D. harmless bacteria are destroyed

15. Orange juice prepared the night before it is to be served should be stored

    A. in a container that will protect it from exposure to air
    B. at 32° F
    C. at 70° F
    D. in a plastic shaker-type container

16. When food has been spilled on an electric cooking element,

    A. clean immediately
    B. wash with soap and water when cool
    C. clean with steel wool
    D. clean with a dry brush after food chars

17. Pork should always be cooked to the well-done state in order to

    A. develop the best possible flavor
    B. prevent trichinosis in the consumer
    C. improve the tenderness
    D. prevent loss of nutritives in juices

18. To prevent curdling of mayonnaise,

    A. expose to light
    B. expose to air
    C. store at 32° F
    D. store at 150° F

19. To avoid the development of bacterial toxins in custards and cream pies, one should

    A. cool to room temperature before refrigeration
    B. refrigerate within half hour after cooking
    C. heat to 212° F during cooking
    D. store in the freezing compartment

20. An excellent medium for the growth of bacteria which cause food poisoning toxins is

    A. cream puffs
    B. pickled watermelon rind
    C. nougat candies
    D. preserves

21. The flavor of fruit is due to

    A. its color pigmentation
    B. citric and malic acids
    C. inorganic salts
    D. pectins

22. Which of the following is used to ripen fruits and vegetables?

    A. Chlorophyll
    B. Methylene
    C. Ethylene
    D. Benzoate of soda

23. Of the following, the BEST selection of orange for making orange juice is the

    A. Rome Beauty
    B. Navel
    C. Valencia
    D. Macintosh

24. To preserve the shape, fruits should be cooked

    A. without sugar
    B. with very little sugar
    C. by adding sugar after cooking
    D. by adding sugar before cooking

25. A prolific source of pectin for use in industry is

    A. fruits
    B. carrots
    C. walnuts
    D. calves' knuckles

26. Substances in fruits and vegetables which are responsible for the ripening process are

    A. molds   B. yeasts   C. bacteria   D. enzymes

27. Sulfuring dried fruits

    A. promotes retention of vitamin B
    B. prevents darkening
    C. activates vitamin C
    D. increases tenderness

28. Little spoilage occurs in stored, sun-dried fruits because the

   A. micro-organisms have been destroyed
   B. moisture content is low
   C. pectin is inactive
   D. yeasts do not flourish in the absence of light

29. Tenderized dried fruits have been

   A. sulphurized, dried, then partially cooked
   B. dried, partially cooked, then partially dried
   C. partially cooked, dried, then partially cooked
   D. dried, sulphurized, then partially cooked

30. Salted fish roe is sold as

   A. macedoine   B. curry   C. brioche   D. caviar

31. Aerobic bacteria which cause food spoilage

   A. are unable to grow without air
   B. are able to grow without air
   C. grow equally well with or without air
   D. need heat and moisture for growth

32. For everyday use, the Fahrenheit temperature of the refrigerator should be

   A. 20-25°   B. 35-40°   C. 45-50°   D. 55-60°

33. Incompletely cooked pork, if eaten, may result in

   A. botulism   B. ptomaine
   C. trichinosis   D. typhoid

34. The process which makes it possible to store fresh food in any climate without refrigeration for an unlimited length of time is

   A. dehydration   B. freezing
   C. freeze-drying   D. flake-drying

35. Frozen foods deteriorate in flavor unless they are kept at

   A. 32° F   B. 32° C   C. 0° F   D. 0° C

KEY (CORRECT ANSWERS)

1.	C	16.	D
2.	A	17.	B
3.	D	18.	A
4.	B	19.	B
5.	B	20.	A
6.	A	21.	D
7.	C	22.	C
8.	A	23.	C
9.	C	24.	D
10.	B	25.	A
11.	B	26.	D
12.	A	27.	B
13.	A	28.	B
14.	C	29.	B
15.	A	30.	D
31.	A		
32.	B		
33.	C		
34.	C		
35.	C		

EXAMINATION SECTION
TEST 1

DIRECTIONS: Each question or incomplete statement is followed by several suggested answers or completions. Select the one that BEST answers the question or completes the statement. *PRINT THE LETTER OF THE CORRECT ANSWER IN THE SPACE AT THE RIGHT.*

1. An experiment was conducted in which juice was extracted from an infected tobacco plant and passes through a porcelain filter.
   When this juice was brought into contact with a healthy tobacco plant and caused the same disease, the experiment led to the discovery of

   A. bacteria B. protozoa
   C. viruses   D. cancer cells

   1.____

2. A genetic variation in which a new gene takes over the locus of the old is referred to as a(n)

   A. aberration   B. mutation
   C. translocation D. deficiency

   2.____

3. When black, rough-coated guinea pigs, hybrid for both color and texture of coat, are crossed, some of their offspring are white, smooth-coated guinea pigs.
   This is a classic illustration of the law of

   A. independent assortment B. dominance
   C. linkage   D. segregation

   3.____

4. Which one of the following receptors is INCORRECTLY paired with the structure in which it is found?

   A. Taste bud - Tongue
   B. Rod - Retina
   C. Cone - Retina
   D. Proprioceptor - Nasal epithelium

   4.____

5. A gland which acts both as a duct gland as well as a ductless gland is the

   A. thyroid   B. adrenal
   C. parathyroid D. pancreas

   5.____

6. A vitamin formerly thought to be a simple compound but now known to be a complex of at least ten separate vitamins is vitamin

   A. A   B. B   C. C   D. D

   6.____

7. Of the following nutrients, the one which is absorbed by the lymph, rather than by the blood in the capillaries, is

   A. amino acids B. fatty acids
   C. glucose   D. water

   7.____

8. A person of type AB blood should be given a transfusion

   A. only from O and AB   B. only from AB and A
   C. only from AB and B   D. from either O, A, B, or AB

   8.____

29

9. A classic study on human gastric digestion was performed by

   A. Beaumont   B. Schleiden   C. Pavlov   D. Banting

10. The nervous system is derived from

    A. ectoderm
    B. mesoderm
    C. endoderm
    D. a combination of endoderm and ectoderm

11. Which one of the following series is in the CORRECT sequence?

    A. Fertilized egg, cleavage, blastula, gastrula
    B. Blastula, fertilized egg, gastrula, cleavage
    C. Blastula, cleavage, gastrula, fertilized egg
    D. Fertilized egg, blastula, cleavage, gastrula

12. Which one of the following statements regarding plant hormones is NOT true?

    A. Despite much research, auxins have thus far not been synthesized.
    B. The auxins from an oat coleoptile can be absorbed on a block of agar and used for further experimentation.
    C. Auxins accelerate lengthwise growth in the stem.
    D. Auxins retard lengthwise growth in the root.

13. In a woody stem, all growth results from the activity of the

    A. cambium   B. phloem   C. pith   D. xylem

14. Which one of the following pairs is INCORRECTLY matched?

    A. Strawberry - eyes   B. Raspberry - layers
    C. Onion - bulbs   D. Potato - tubers

15. It was a relatively simple task for Mendel to secure pure lines in the garden pea since in nature it is _____ pollinated.

    A. wind   B. insect   C. water   D. self

16. Respiration in plants is

    A. similar to respiration in animals and takes place at all times
    B. similar to respiration in animals and takes place only when the plant is not carrying on photosynthesis
    C. different from respiration in animals and takes place at all times
    D. different from respiration in animals and takes place only when the plant is not carrying on photo-synthesis

17. Modern research indicates that photosynthesis consists

    A. only of rapid light reactions
    B. only of slow light reactions
    C. only of a dark reaction
    D. of a light reaction followed by a dark reaction

18. Cells obtain energy quickly through

    A. photosynthesis
    B. oxidation of glucose
    C. hydrolysis of ATP
    D. osmosis

19. Which one of the following statements with regard to enzymes is NOT true?

    A. Enzymes are organic catalysts produced by living cells
    B. Enzymes are specific, frequently acting only upon a single substrate.
    C. An enzyme can accelerate a specific reaction in only one direction.
    D. Enzymes have a protein component.

20. A reduction division takes place

    A. only in animal cells during mitosis
    B. only in plant cells during mitosis
    C. in both plant and animal cells during mitosis
    D. in both plant and animal cells during meiosis

21. The essential determiner of heredity in every living cell is a substance known as

    A. DNA   B. ACTH   C. 2-4D   D. ATP

22. If the number of protons in the nucleus of each atom is the same as the number in every other atom, the substance is

    A. inert
    B. an active non-metal
    C. amphoteric
    D. an element

23. Of the following atomic particles, the LIGHTEST in weight is the

    A. proton
    B. electron
    C. alpha particle
    D. neutron

24. The PRINCIPAL difference between a mixture and a chemical compound is that a

    A. mixture is always heterogeneous in composition
    B. mixture does not contain chemical substances
    C. compound is always of definite composition
    D. compound is more easily separated into its constituent parts

25. Boiling is an effective method of purifying water that contains

    A. soluble organic impurities
    B. bacteria and dissolved gases
    C. insoluble inorganic impurities
    D. soluble organic impurities and bacteria

KEY (CORRECT ANSWERS)

1. C
2. B
3. A
4. D
5. D

6. B
7. B
8. D
9. A
10. A

11. A
12. A
13. A
14. A
15. D

16. A
17. D
18. C
19. C
20. D

21. A
22. D
23. B
24. C
25. B

TEST 2

DIRECTIONS: Each question or incomplete statement is followed by several suggested answers or completions. Select the one that BEST answers the question or completes the statement. *PRINT THE LETTER OF THE CORRECT ANSWER IN THE SPACE AT THE RIGHT.*

1. An inexpensive, readily available raw material for the chemical manufacture of washing soda, hydrochloric acid and chlorine, is

    A. NaCl
    B. Na_2CO_3
    C. HCl
    D. $Na_2CO_3 10H_2O$

    1.____

2. About 75% of the air by weight is

    A. carbon dioxide
    B. argon
    C. oxygen
    D. nitrogen

    2.____

3. Argon gas is used to fill tungsten filament electric light bulbs because it

    A. supports the combustion of the filament
    B. offers less resistance to the flow of current than nitrogen
    C. is inert and slows the evaporation of the filament
    D. is less expensive than pure oxygen

    3.____

4. The number of sub atomic particles that have been identi-fied are

    A. ten
    B. twenty-five
    C. fifty
    D. one hundred

    4.____

5. In ordinary chemical reactions, atoms combine with each other when

    A. electrons are transferred from one atom to another
    B. nuclear particles are shared
    C. one atom loses protons gained by the other
    D. the transfer of particles produces ions with no electrical charge

    5.____

6. Adenine, thymine, cytosine, and guanine are ALL

    A. chemical names for common vitamins
    B. units that constitute the genetic code of DNA
    C. important hormones
    D. enzymes active in digestion

    6.____

7. A gas distributed commercially in solid form for use as a refrigerant is

    A. chlorine
    B. carbon dioxide
    C. argon
    D. nitrogen

    7.____

8. Paraffin wax used to make candles is obtained commercially by

    A. the cracking of kerosene
    B. the hydrogenation of fuel oil
    C. the fractional distillation of crude oil
    D. polymerization of pure hydrocarbons

    8.____

9. The E.M.F. that pushes electrons through an electrical circuit is measured in

    A. ohms   B. volts   C. coulombs   D. amperes

10. The north pole of a compass needle will often point slightly away from true north because the

    A. compass needle does not line up with the magnetic lines of force of the earth
    B. North Star is not an accurate reference point for determining true north
    C. magnetic pole and the geographic pole of the earth do not coincide
    D. position of the geographic North Pole is not definite

11. If 1 quart of water at $100°$ C is added to 1 gallon of water at $0°$ C, the number of calories gained by the colder water as compared with the number of calories lost by the warmer water is as

    A. 1:1   B. 1:4   C. 4:1   D. 0.25:1

12. A bobsled track is banked at the turns in order to over-come

    A. drag   B. centrifugal force
    C. friction   D. gravity

13. In Einstein's formula $E = MC^2$, the factor E = energy, M = mass, and C represents

    A. the speed of light
    B. Hooke's constant
    C. the Lorentz transformation factor
    D. Planck's constant

14. A solid cube will float in water if the

    A. weight of the water it displaces is less than the weight of the cube
    B. water density is greater than the density of the cube
    C. water has expanded due to heating
    D. difference in weight between the cube and an equal volume of water is less than 1 gm.

15. A block will slide with uniform velocity down an inclined plane when the frictional resistance to its motion is

    A. ignored
    B. increased slightly
    C. equal to the force pulling it down the plane
    D. slightly greater than the force pulling it down the plane

16. The differential gears on the rear axle of an automobile

    A. shift when the automatic transmission shifts
    B. enable the driver to obtain maximum speeds with minimum consumption of gasoline
    C. make it possible to use one non-skid chain effectively instead of two
    D. permit one wheel to travel faster than the other on curves

17. The laser is a device which produces light amplification through stimulated 17.____

   A. electrical reactance
   B. induced magnetism
   C. emission radiation
   D. frequency modulation

18. Nearsightedness is GENERALLY corrected by using a 18.____

   A. converging lens
   B. convex lens
   C. concave lens
   D. lens of focal length 13 mm.

19. If there are 4 supporting strands in the pulley system, a 400 lb. safe can be lifted (neglecting friction) by applying a force of _____ lbs. 19.____

   A. 32   B. 40   C. 100   D. 400

20. When currents are set up in a liquid through unequal heating, the heat is transferred PRINCIPALLY by 20.____

   A. conduction
   B. radiation
   C. vapor pressure
   D. convection

21. Which one of the following is NOT a recommended soil erosion control measure? 21.____

   A. Terracing
   B. Crop rotation
   C. Strip cropping
   D. Plowing instead of burning stubble

22. Which one of the following statements is TRUE of contour maps? 22.____

   A. The closer the contour lines, the steeper the grade.
   B. The more separated the contour lines, the steeper the grade.
   C. When contour lines become too close to distinguish, a smaller contour interval is used.
   D. Contour lines represent relief better than hachures do.

23. A very meandering course, flat topography with no falls or rapids, poor drainage on the flood plain, swampy vegetation and few tributaries are characteristic of a river in its 23.____

   A. youth
   B. maturity
   C. old age
   D. maturity and old age

24. Potholes, outwash plains, hanging valleys, and kames are all terms DIRECTLY associated with the activities of 24.____

   A. rivers   B. glaciers   C. volcanoes   D. mountains

25. Which one of the following statements with regard to cyclones is NOT true? 25.____

   A. Hurricanes are tropical cyclones.
   B. The air in a cyclone moves rapidly outward from the *eye*.
   C. Sooner or later, all cyclones conform to the path of the prevailing westerlies.
   D. A cyclone is merely a low pressure area and the winds within it may have any velocity.

KEY (CORRECT ANSWERS)

1.	A	11.	A
2.	D	12.	B
3.	C	13.	A
4.	D	14.	B
5.	A	15.	C
6.	B	16.	D
7.	B	17.	C
8.	C	18.	C
9.	B	19.	C
10.	C	20.	D

21. B
22. A
23. C
24. B
25. B

TEST 3

DIRECTIONS: Each question or incomplete statement is followed by several suggested answers or completions. Select the one that BEST answers the question or completes the statement. *PRINT THE LETTER OF THE CORRECT ANSWER IN THE SPACE AT THE RIGHT.*

1. The gland which produces insulin is to be found in the   1._____

    A. liver   B. pituitary   C. thymus   D. pancreas

2. Gamma globulins used in the protection against measles and polio contain   2._____

    A. toxoids   B. dead viruses
    C. weakened viruses   D. antibodies

3. Low sodium diets are used for the   3._____

    A. prevention of edema
    B. treatment of heart disease
    C. reduction of cholesterol in the blood
    D. treatment of bacterial endocarditis

4. Of the following diseases, the one whose causative agent is of a different type from those of the other three is   4._____

    A. diphtheria   B. tetanus
    C. poliomyelitis   D. typhoid fever

5. *Do not move the patient* is a first aid precept which is applicable particularly in cases of   5._____

    A. bleeding and fainting   B. fracture and shock
    C. sunstroke and asphyxia   D. burns and heat exhaustion

6. All of the following statements pertaining to items found in home medicine cabinets are correct EXCEPT: 6._____

    A. Tincture of iodine is unaffected by long storage and hence may be used indefinitely
    B. Hydrogen peroxide is usable as long as it bubbles energetically
    C. Age does not make sedatives dangerous, but they may lose some of their potency with time
    D. If the supply of bicarbonate of soda is exhausted, baking soda may be substituted

7. Of the following, the INCORRECT association of a disease with the period of time during which it is usually communicable is   7._____

    A. impetigo - as long as the sores are unhealed
    B. measles - during the period of running eyes and nose
    C. diphtheria - usually two weeks from the onset of the infection
    D. tetanus - from the onset of the disease to one week later

8. The group of terms which is correctly arranged in the order of increasing inclusiveness, the LEAST inclusive being stated first, is   8._____

    A. tissues, cells, systems, organs
    B. cells, organs, tissues, organisms
    C. cells, genes, organs, tissues
    D. cells, tissues, organs, systems

9. Ascorbic acid is a vitamin whose presence in foods prevents the occurrence of
   A. beriberi
   B. night blindness
   C. scurvy
   D. rickets

10. Vitamin A deficiency is associated with all of the following EXCEPT
    A. faulty development of the teeth
    B. impairment of vision in dim light
    C. unhealthy condition of the skin and mucous membranes
    D. retardation of the development of bones

11. Aureomycin was developed by
    A. Fleming   B. Banting   C. Waksman   D. Duggar

12. A class of engines that are NOT of the internal combustion type is _____ engines.
    A. diesel
    B. gasoline
    C. turbo-jet
    D. steam

13. The lead storage battery commonly used in American auto-mobiles is filled with a solution of _____ acid.
    A. sulfuric
    B. nitric
    C. phosphoric
    D. hydrochloric

14. All stars visible to the naked eye belong to
    A. the solar system
    B. a number of galaxies
    C. the Milky Way galaxy
    D. the Milky Way galaxy and several spiral nebulae

15. A poisonous snake native to the eastern United States is the
    A. puff adder
    B. king snake
    C. milk snake
    D. water moccasin

16. When an observer hears thunder 10 seconds after he sees the lightning flash that caused it, the distance between him and the point of origin of the flash is APPROXIMATELY _____ mile(s).
    A. 1   B. 2   C. 5   D. 10

17. Rivers flowing into a lake may eventually destroy it by
    A. erosion
    B. stream piracy
    C. deposition
    D. solution

18. The metal used for the filament of the modern incandescent lamp is
    A. tungsten   B. tantalum   C. thorium   D. titanium

19. The APPROXIMATE number of miles per degree of latitude of the earth is
    A. 90   B. 70   C. 15
    D. widely variable, depending on location

20. The bedrock of a large part of Manhattan is the rock called 20._____
    A. granite   B. quartzite   C. schist   D. trap

21. The function of the cadmium rods in a nuclear reactor is to _____ neutrons. 21._____
    A. slow down   B. absorb   C. speed up   D. create

22. The BRIGHTEST star visible in the nightime sky in New York City is 22._____
    A. Betelgeuse   B. Orion   C. Polaris   D. Sirius

23. A dry cleaning fluid which is NOT flammable is 23._____
    A. carbon disulfide   B. carbon tetrachloride
    C. dimethyl phthalate   D. freon

24. The dark gray clouds that form a complete overcast on rainy days are called 24._____
    A. alto-stratus   B. nimbo-stratus
    C. cumulus   D. cirrus

25. Most of the United States lies in the terrestrial wind belt affected by the prevailing 25._____
    A. southwesterlies   B. northwesterlies
    C. southeasterlies   D. northeasterlies

KEY (CORRECT ANSWERS)

1. D   11. D
2. D   12. D
3. A   13. A
4. C   14. C
5. B   15. D

6. A   16. B
7. D   17. C
8. D   18. A
9. C   19. B
10. D   20. D

21. B
22. D
23. B
24. B
25. A

TEST 4

DIRECTIONS: Each question or incomplete statement is followed by several suggested answers or completions. Select the one that BEST answers the question or completes the statement. *PRINT THE LETTER OF THE CORRECT ANSWER IN THE SPACE AT THE RIGHT.*

1. In general, as latitude increases from 0° to about 30°, precipitation
   - A. remains uniform
   - B. increases
   - C. decreases
   - D. shows no particular trend

2. Heavy dew is MOST likely to form on a _____ night.
   - A. calm, clear
   - B. clear, windy
   - C. calm, cloudy
   - D. windy, overcast

3. The Catskill Mountains of New York State can BEST be described as
   - A. coastal plain
   - B. folded mountain
   - C. plateau
   - D. a series of domes

4. Bays like San Francisco Bay, Chesapeake Bay, and Delaware Bay are
   - A. parts of deltas
   - B. fiords
   - C. artificial harbors
   - D. submerged river valleys

5. When first aid is to be administered to a pupil who has been injured in the classroom, of the four measures indicated below, the one which should be given PRECEDENCE is
   - A. controlling the bleeding
   - B. moving the student out of the classroom
   - C. sending for a doctor
   - D. treating for shock

6. The normal number of teeth in the adult human being is
   - A. 28
   - B. 32
   - C. 36
   - D. 30

7. The reproductive organs of a flowering plant are the
   - A. stomata and guard cells
   - B. fibrovascular bundles and sieve tubes
   - C. pistils and stamens
   - D. cambium layer and lenticels

8. A virus is the causative agent of
   - A. malaria
   - B. tetanus
   - C. smallpox
   - D. typhoid fever

9. In a blast furnace, the slag
   - A. is drained off from below the molten iron
   - B. floats on top of the molten iron
   - C. is mixed with the iron to produce steel
   - D. mixes with the iron when the *pigs* form

10. If iron filings are sprinkled on a sheet of paper under which the north poles of two bar magnets face one another at a distance of one and a quarter inches, the lines of force show

    A. repulsion
    B. attraction
    C. partial attraction
    D. irregularities indicating both attraction and repulsion

11. Of the following, the substance which is NOT an antibiotic is

    A. aureomycin
    B. penicillin
    C. streptomycin
    D. sulphanilamide

12. The electric meter in the home measures

    A. kilowatts
    B. kilowatt-hours
    C. watts
    D. watt-hours

13. The blood group which is COMMONLY referred to as the *universal donor* is

    A. A B. B C. AB D. O

14. Renewal of the supply of oxygen in our atmosphere is accomplished CHIEFLY by the

    A. burning of wood and coal that occurs throughout the world
    B. natural decomposition of oxides found in the earth's surface
    C. photosynthetic process in plants
    D. normal loss of dissolved gases from the oceans

15. Mumps is an infection of the

    A. cervical lymph glands
    B. parotid glands
    C. thyroid glands
    D. tonsils

16. Radioactive iodine is used effectively in the treatment of cancer of the

    A. adrenals B. liver C. thymus D. thyroid

17. In television broadcasting, light waves from the subject are changed into electrical impulses by a

    A. converter
    B. detector tube
    C. photoelectric cell
    D. scanning disc

18. The star Polaris is found in the constellation

    A. Arcturus
    B. Big Dipper
    C. Cassiopeia
    D. Little Dipper

19. MOST digested food is absorbed into the bloodstream through the walls of the

    A. large intestine
    B. pancreas
    C. small intestine
    D. stomach

20. To test the strength of the charge of a storage battery, it is BEST to use a(n)

    A. ammeter
    B. hydrometer
    C. neon test lamp
    D. voltmeter

21. A body in motion remains in motion in a straight line at the same rate unless it is acted on by an external disturbing force.
    This is, in part, a statement of the law of
    A. inertia   B. falling bodies
    C. relativity   D. mass action

22. Summer thunderstorms in the northeastern part of the United States are USUALLY associated with _____ clouds.
    A. cirrus   B. cumulus   C. nimbus   D. stratus

23. A plant grower produces a new kind of rose. He can propagate and perpetuate the new rose by
    A. cross-pollination   B. grafting
    C. inbreeding   D. self-pollination

24. A catalyst
    A. alters the rate of chemical change
    B. emulsifies fats
    C. fixes a dye in fabric
    D. is a reducing agent

25. A plant whose seeds are dispersed by the wind is the
    A. burdock   B. coconut
    C. horse chestnut   D. maple

KEY (CORRECT ANSWERS)

1.	C	11.	D
2.	A	12.	B
3.	C	13.	D
4.	D	14.	C
5.	A	15.	B
6.	B	16.	D
7.	C	17.	C
8.	C	18.	D
9.	B	19.	C
10.	A	20.	B

21. A
22. B
23. B
24. A
25. D

TEST 5

DIRECTIONS: Each question or incomplete statement is followed by several suggested answers or completions. Select the one that BEST answers the question or completes the statement. *PRINT THE LETTER OF THE CORRECT ANSWER IN THE SPACE AT THE RIGHT.*

1. Glass is etched by a solution of _____ acid.   1.____
   - A. hydrofluoric
   - B. carbolic
   - C. nitric
   - D. sulfuric

2. The phases of the moon are caused by the   2.____
   - A. earth's revolution
   - B. earth's rotation
   - C. moon's revolution
   - D. moon's rotation

3. The Lysenko theories of inheritance have a CLOSE similarity to the theories of   3.____
   - A. De Vries
   - B. Lamarck
   - C. Mendel
   - D. Galton

4. Vitamin D is found in comparatively large amounts in   4.____
   - A. fish liver oils
   - B. citrus fruits
   - C. leafy vegetables
   - D. lean meats

5. Particularly rich uranium deposits have been found in   5.____
   - A. Belgian Congo
   - B. Iran
   - C. Mexico
   - D. Chile

6. The oceans cover _____ tenths of the surface of the earth.   6.____
   - A. three
   - B. five
   - C. seven
   - D. nine

7. The area of Europe is roughly _____ that of the United States.   7.____
   - A. half
   - B. the same as
   - C. twice
   - D. three times

8. The process LEAST likely to result in vitamin loss is   8.____
   - A. bleaching celery
   - B. refining flour
   - C. quick freezing fruits
   - D. peeling vegetables

9. The natural resource of the United States which it is commonly expected will be FIRST exhausted is   9.____
   - A. iron ore
   - B. coal
   - C. bauxite
   - D. petroleum

10. The SHORTEST distance between any two points on the earth's surface is always along a(n)   10.____
    - A. arc of a meridian
    - B. arc of a parallel of latitude
    - C. arc of a great circle
    - D. contour line

11. Normally, a farm in the temperate zone in order to raise most crops must have a yearly rainfall amounting to at LEAST _____ inches.

   A. 20 B. 40 C. 60 D. 80

12. A good example of a *continental climate* is found in

   A. North Dakota   B. Florida
   C. New York   D. Alaska

13. The word *doldrums* refers to

   A. mountains that are difficult to climb
   B. tropical islands of volcanic origin
   C. geysers that erupt irregularly
   D. parts of the ocean where calms prevail

14. At the time of the vernal equinox (about March 21st), the sun at noon is DIRECTLY over the

   A. Tropic of Capricorn and moving north
   B. Tropic of Cancer and moving south
   C. Equator and moving north
   D. Equator and moving south

15. New Year's Day will be celebrated FIRST in

   A. New York   B. Rome   C. Bombay   D. Manila

16. Of the following sources of energy, the one which appears NOT to be exploitation of the energy radiated by the sun is

   A. coal   B. organic food
   C. tidal power D. water power

17. Lime is used

   A. in blast furnaces
   B. in manufacturing cement
   C. in the production of carbonated drinks
   D. for reducing the acidity of the soil

18. An appliance in which chemical energy is changed into electrical energy is a

   A. galvanometer   B. hydrometer
   C. storage battery D. thermocouple

19. Galileo noticed that black spots crossed the visible solar disc in about fourteen days. This shows that

   A. the sun rotates in about twenty-seven days
   B. the sun rotates in about fourteen days
   C. there are cyclonic storms in the sun's atmosphere somewhat like the cyclonic storms on the earth in the area of the westerlies
   D. there are volcanic craters on the sun which gradually shift their position

20. The set of prisms incorporated in a pair of field glasses   20.____

    A. changes the light path B. increases the illumination
    C. inverts the image D. reflects the image

21. Attempts have been made to improve the genetic make-up of the human race by   21.____

    A. adopting social security laws
    B. improving the food habits of large numbers of people
    C. providing better housing
    D. sterilizing the feeble-minded

22. The part of the seedless grape plant that is used in producing more seedless grape plants is the   22.____

    A. fruit B. leaf C. root D. stem

23. Evergreen trees whose needles grow in clusters are   23.____

    A. balsams B. hemlocks C. pines D. spruces

24. Data concerning the entire surface of the moon are NOT available because   24.____

    A. telescopes are not yet powerful enough
    B. the half of the moon which faces the earth in the daytime is not visible at night
    C. the period of rotation of the moon is exactly the same as its period of revolution
    D. until very recently radar contact with the moon had not yet been made

25. The FIRST cyclotron was devised by   25.____

    A. E.O. Lawrence B. Lise Meitner
    C. Robert Oppenheimer D. Hugh Taylor

KEY (CORRECT ANSWERS)

1. A
2. C
3. B
4. A
5. A

6. C
7. B
8. C
9. D
10. C

11. A
12. A
13. D
14. C
15. D

16. C
17. D
18. C
19. A
20. D

21. D
22. D
23. C
24. C
25. A

EXAMINATION SECTION
TEST 1

DIRECTIONS: Each question or incomplete statement is followed by several suggested answers or completions. Select the one that BEST answers the question or completes the statement. *PRINT THE LETTER OF THE CORRECT ANSWER IN THE SPACE AT THE RIGHT.*

Questions 1-7.

DIRECTIONS: Questions 1 through 7 refer to the diagram that follows. Base your choice on the information given in the selection and on your own understanding of science.

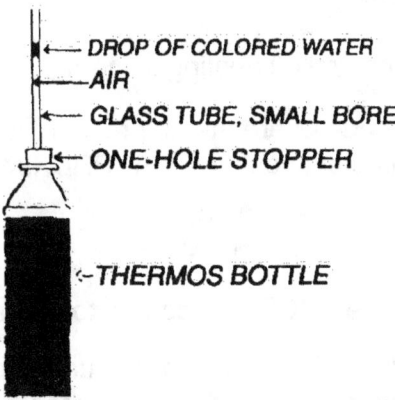

1. The device shown in the diagram above indicates changes that are measured MORE accurately by a(n)

   A. thermometer   B. hygrometer   C. anemometer
   D. hydrometer   E. barometer

1._____

2. If the device is placed in a cold refrigerator for 72 hours, which of the following is MOST likely to happen?

   A. The stopper will be forced out of the bottle.
   B. The drop of water will evaporate.
   C. the drop will move downward.
   D. The drop will move upward.
   E. No change will take place

2._____

3. When the device was carried in an elevator from the first floor to the sixth floor of a building, the drop of colored water moved about 1/4 inch in the tube. Which of the following is MOST probably true?

   A. The drop moved downward because there was a decrease in the air pressure.
   B. The drop moved upward because there was a decrease in the air pressure.
   C. The drop moved downward because there was an increase in the air temperature.
   D. The drop moved upward because there was an increase in the air temperature.
   E. The drop moved downward because there was an increase in the temperature and a decrease in the pressure.

3._____

47

4. The part of a thermos bottle into which liquids are poured consists of

   A. a single-walled, metal flask coated with silver
   B. two flasks, one of glass and one of silvered metal
   C. two silvered-glass flasks separated by a vacuum
   D. two silver flasks separated by a vacuum
   E. a single-walled glass flask with a silver-colored coating

5. The thermos bottle is MOST similar in principle to

   A. the freezing unit in an electric refrigerator
   B. radiant heaters
   C. solar heating systems
   D. storm windows
   E. a thermostatically controlled heating system

6. In a plane flying at an altitude where the air pressure is only half the normal pressure at sea level, the plane's altimeter should read APPROXIMATELY

   A. 3,000 feet   B. 9,000 feet   C. 18,000 feet
   D. 27,000 feet E. 60,000 feet

7. Which of the following is the POOREST conductor of heat?

   A. Air under a pressure of 1.5 pounds per square inch
   B. Air under a pressure of 15 pounds per square inch
   C. Unsilvered glass
   D. Silvered glass
   E. Silver

Questions 8-17.

DIRECTIONS: Questions 8 through 17 refer to the passage that follows. Base your choice on the information given in the passage *and on your own understanding of the subject.*

The formed elements of the blood are the red corpuscles or erythrocytes, the white corpuscles or leucocytes, the blood platelets, and the so-called blood dust or hemoconiae. Together, these constitute 30-40 percent by volume of the whole blood, the remainder being taken up by the plasma. In man, there are normally 5,000,000 red cells per cubic millimeter of blood; the count is somewhat lower in women. Variations occur frequently, especially after exercise or a heavy meal, or at high altitudes. Except in camels, which have elliptical corpuscles, the shape of the mammalian corpuscle is that of a circular, nonnucleated, bi-concave disk. The average diameter usually given is 7.7 microns, a value obtained by examining dried preparations of blood and considered by Ponder to be too low. Ponder's own observations, made on red cells in the fresh state, show the human corpuscle to have an average diameter of 8.8 microns. When circulating in the blood vessels, the red cell does not maintain a fixed shape but changes its form constantly, especially in the small capillaries. The red blood corpuscles are continually undergoing destruction, new corpuscles being formed to replace them. The average life of red corpuscles has been estimated by various investigators to be between three and six weeks. Preceding destruction, changes in the composition of the cells are believed to occur which render them less resistant. In the process of destruction, the lipids of the membrane are dissolved and the hemoglobin which is liberated is the most important, though probably not the only source of bilirubin. The belief that the liver is the only site of red celldestruction is no longer generally held. The leucocytes, of which there are several forms, usually number 7000 and 9000 per cubic millimeter of blood. These increase in number in disease, particularly when there is bacterial infection.

8. Leukemia is a disease involving the

    A. red cells   B. white cells   C. plasma
    D. blood platelets   E. blood dust

8.____

9. "The erythrocytes in the blood are increased in number after a heavy meal." The paragraph implies that this

    A. is true   B. holds only for camels
    C. is not true   D. may be true
    E. depends on the number of white cells

9.____

10. When blood is dried, the red cells

    A. contract   B. remain the same size   C. disintegrate
    D. expand   E. become elliptical

10.____

11. Ponder is PROBABLY classified as a professional

    A. pharmacist   B. physicist   C. psychologist
    D. physiologist   E. psychiatrist

11.____

12. The term *erythema* when applied to skin conditions signifies

    A. redness   B. swelling   C. irritation
    D. pain   E. roughness

12.____

13. Lipids are insoluble in water and soluble in such solvents as ether, chloroform and benzene. It may be inferred that the membrane of red cells MOST closely resemble

    A. egg white   B. sugar   C. bone   D. butter
    E. cotton fiber

13.____

14. Analysis of a sample of blood yields cell counts of 4,800,000 erythrocytes and 16,000 leucocytes per cubic millimeter. These data suggest that the patient from whom the blood was taken

    A. is anemic
    B. has been injuriously invaded by germs
    C. has been exposed to high-pressure air
    D. has a normal cell count
    E. has lost a great deal of blood

14.____

15. Bilirubin, a bile pigment, is

    A. an end product of several different reactions
    B. formed only in the liver
    C. formed from the remnants of the dell membranes of erythrocytes
    D. derived from hemoglobin exclusively
    E. a precursor of hemoglobin

15.____

16. Bancroft found that the blood count of the natives in the Peruvian Andes differed from that usually accepted as normal. The blood PROBABLY differed in respect to

    A. leucocytes   B. blood platelets   C. cell shapes
    D. erythrocytes   E. hemoconiae

17. Hemoglobin is probably NEVER found

    A. free in the blood stream   B. in the red cells
    C. in women's blood   D. in the blood after exercise
    E. in the leucocytes

Questions 18-27.

DIRECTIONS: Questions 18 through 27 refer to the passage that follows. Base your choice on the information given in the passage *and on your own understanding of the subject.*

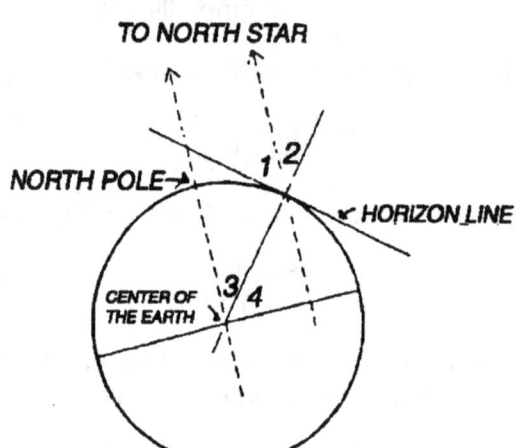

    The latitude of any point on the earth's surface is the angle between a plumb line dropped to the center of the earth from that point and the plane of the earth's equator. Since it is impossible to go to the center of the earth to measure latitude, the latitude of any point may be determined indirectly as shown in the accompanying diagram.
    It will be recalled that the axis of the earth, if extended outward, passes very near the North Star. Since the North Star is, for all practical purposes, infinitely distant, the line of sight to the North Star of an observer on the surface of the earth is virtually parallel with the earth's axis. Angle 1, then, in the diagram represents the angular distance of the North Star above the horizon. Angle 2 is equal to angle 3, because when two parallel lines are intersected by a straight line, the corresponding angles are equal. Angle 1 plus angle 2 is a right angle and so is angle 3 plus angle 4. Therefore, angle 1 equals angle 4 because when equals are subtracted from equals the results are equal.

18. If an observer finds that the angular distance of the North Star above the horizon is 30, his latitude is

    A. 15° N   B. 30° N   C. 60° N   D. 90° N   E. 120° N

19. To an observer on the equator, the North Star would be 19.____

   A. 30° above the horizon
   B. 60° above the horizon
   C. 90° above the horizon
   D. on the horizon
   E. below the horizon

20. To an observer on the Arctic Circle, the North Star would be 20.____

   A. directly overhead
   B. 23 1/2° above the horizon
   C. 66 1/2° above the horizon
   D. on the horizon
   E. below the horizon

21. The distance around the earth along a certain parallel of latitude is 3,600 miles. At this latitude, how many miles are there in one degree of longitude? 21.____

   A. 1 mile
   B. 10 miles
   C. 30 miles
   D. 69 miles
   E. 100 miles

22. At which of the following latitudes would the sun be directly overhead at noon on June 21? 22.____

   A. 0°   B. 23 1/2° S   C. 23 1/2° N   D. 66 1/2° N   E. 66 1/2° S

23. On March 21 the number of hours of daylight at places on the Arctic Circle is 23.____

   A. none   B. 8   C. 12   D. 16   E. 24

24. The distance from the equator to the 45th parallel, measured along a meridian, is APPROXIMATELY 24.____

   A. 450 miles
   B. 900 miles
   C. 1,250 miles
   D. 3,125 miles
   E. 6,250 miles

25. The difference in time between the meridians that pass through longitude 45°E and longitude 105°W is 25.____

   A. 6 hours
   B. 2 hours
   C. 8 hours
   D. 4 hours
   E. 10 hours

26. Which of the following is NOT a great circle or part of a great circle? 26.____

   A. Arctic Circle   B. 100th meridian   C. equator
   D. Shortest distance between New York and London
   E. Greenwich meridian

27. At which of the following places does the sun set earliest on June 21? 27.____

   A. Montreal, Canada
   B. Santiago, Chile
   C. Mexico City, Mexico
   D. Lima, Peru
   E. Manila, P.I.

28. At which of the following cities is the daily temperature range GREATEST? 28.____

   A. Key West
   B. Los Angeles
   C. Chicago
   D. New York City
   E. Denver

29. The MAXIMUM percentage of water vapor possible in the air is about 29.____

   A. 1%   B. 78%   C. .03%   D. 4%   E. 100%

30. When a mass of air rises, it is cooled CHIEFLY because

   A. it expands
   B. moisture condenses
   C. ice crystals are formed
   D. it mixes with cold air
   E. it is closer to cold outer space

31. An amateur pilot flying into a series of cold front thunderstorms should

   A. fly through without change of course
   B. fly around the thunderstorms
   C. land and get his plane into a hangar
   D. fly under the storm front
   E. fly over the top

32. Soaring pilots find MOST thermals

   A. about midmorning
   B. about 2 hours after noon
   C. in late afternoon
   D. Just after sunset
   E. in early morning

33. On a contour map, lines that are close together indicate that the land

   A. slopes gently   B. is swampy   C. slopes steeply
   D. is high   E. is impassable

34. The planet that is NEAREST in size to the Earth is

   A. Mars   B. Venus   C. Mercury   D. Uranus   E. Jupiter

35. Of the total mass of the sun, planets, moons and other bodies in our solar system, the sun comprises APPROXIMATELY

   A. 1%   B. 10%   C. 50%   D. 90%   E. 99%

36. A sea cave at an altitude of 100 feet would indicate

   A. great tidal range
   B. severe storms
   C. uplift of land
   D. submergence of land
   E. rapid deposition of sediment

37. The element that makes up about 50% of the earth's crust is

   A. silicon   B. nitrogen   C. iron
   D. aluminum   E. oxygen

38. Two elements obtained from the sea in commercial quantities are

   A. iron and sulfur
   B. nitrogen and argon
   C. copper and tin
   D. aluminum and iodine
   E. magnesium and bromine

39. Atoms of plutonium are composed of

   A. neutrons and protons
   B. electrons and neutrons
   C. electrons, neutrons and ions
   D. ions, protons and electrons
   E. neutrons, electrons and protons

40. Uranium used in making atomic bombs occurs in the mineral 40.____

   A. hematite B. pitchblende C. franklinite
   D. malachite E. smithsonite

41. Which of the following is an explosive mixture? 41.____

   A. Oxygen and carbon monoxide
   B. Oxygen and caron dioxide
   C. Carbon dioxide and caron monoxide
   D. Carbon dioxide and hydrogen
   E. Nitrogen and carbon dioxide

42. Which of the following will react with baking soda to produce carbon dioxide? 42.____

   A. Table salt B. Cane molasses C. Granulated sugar
   D. Sweet cream E. Wheat flour

43. Which of the following mechanisms requires NO external supply of oxygen? 43.____

   A. Diesel engines B. Four-cycle gasoline engines
   C. Jet turbine engines D. Rockets
   E. Two-cycle internal-combustion engines

44. In an operating radio tube the electrons flow from 44.____

   A. plate to grid B. grid to plate
   C. plate to filament D. filament to plate
   E. grid to filament

45. In hydroelectric stations, the energy of the turbines is applied directly to the operation of 45.____

   A. synchronous motors B. water motors C. steam engines
   D. generators E. electric motors

46. A boy is given two similar bars of iron, which we shall call A and B. He finds that either 46.____
    end of A clings to either end of B, that either end of A clings to the middle of B and that
    neither end of B clings to the middle of A. He concludes CORRECTLY that

   A. both A and B are magnetized
   B. A is magnetized and B is not
   C. B is magnetized and A is not
   D. neither A nor B is magnetized
   E. B is magnetized over its entire length and A is not magnetized in the middle

47. Inductive reaoning is reasoning 47.____

   A. by analogy to similar situations
   B. from faulty premises
   C. after an event has taken place
   D. from a principle to a conclusion
   E. from observations to generalizations

48. If a coin is held 2 feet from an electric lamp, the shadow of the coin 6 feet from the lamp 48.____
    has an area that compares to the area of the coin as

   A. 12 to 1 B. 24 to 1 C. 3 to 1 D. 6 to 1 E. 9 to 1

49. The appliance cord for an electric flatiron is made of

    A. stranded copper wire covered with asbestos and rubber
    B. solid copper wire covered with asbestos and rubber
    C. rubber-covered stranded copper wire
    D. asbestos-covered nichrome wire
    E. rubber-covered nichrome wire

49._____

50. The distributor in an automobile engine controls the

    A. proportion of the electric current flowing to the lights and starter
    B. amount of electric current released from the storage battery
    C. flow of gasoline to the carburetor
    D. transmission of the spark occurrence to the spark plug
    E. amount of pressure on each brake drum

50._____

KEY (CORRECT ANSWERS)

1. A	11. D	21. B	31. C	41. A
2. C	12. A	22. C	32. C	42. D
3. B	13. D	23. C	33. C	43. D
4. C	14. B	24. D	34. B	44. D
5. D	15. A	25. E	35. E	45. D
6. C	16. D	26. A	36. C	46. B
7. A	17. E	27. B	37. E	47. E
8. B	18. B	28. E	38. E	48. E
9. D	19. D	29. D	39. E	49. A
10. A	20. C	30. A	40. B	50. D

TEST 2

DIRECTIONS: Each question or incomplete statement is followed by several suggested answers or completions. Select the one that BEST answers the question or completes the statement. *PRINT THE LETTER OF THE CORRECT ANSWER IN THE SPACE AT THE RIGHT.*

Questions 1-7.

DIRECTIONS: Questions 1 through 7 refer to the diagram that follows. Base your choice on the information given in the selection and on your own understanding of science.

1. The ignition coil in an automobile

   A. regulates the flow of current to the lights
   B. increases the voltage of the current to the spark plugs
   C. controls the charging rate of the battery
   D. boosts the voltage between the battery and the starting motor
   E. takes the place of the generator when the engine is not running

1.____

2. When the gears of an automobile are shifted from "high" to "low," the

   A. power of the motor is increased
   B. force applied by the driving wheels is increased
   C. force applied by the motor is decreased
   D. speed of the driving wheels is increased
   E. transmission gears have increased the power

2.____

3. If metal pipe is to be used to carry liquids or gases, the threaded portion is ALWAYS

   A. straight   B. tapered   C. fine   D. coarse   E. square

3.____

4. Which of these fastening devices is a rivet?

   A.   B.   C.   D.   E.

4.____

5. A substance mixed with cement and water to form the finishing coat on a concrete sidewalk is

   A. fill   B. sand   C. plaster of paris   D. mortar   E. gravel

5.____

6. The board of fire underwriters requires inspection of

   A. house paint   B. roofing material
   C. furnace installation D. hot-water pipes
   E. electric wiring

6.____

7. Which tool is MOST generally used with a brace to bore a hole?

   A. Twist drill   B. Center drill   C. Countersink
   D. Auger bit   E. Rose reamer

7.____

55

8. By what name is this tool commonly called?

   A. Nail set   B. Wedge   C. Pry bar   D. Cold chisel
   E. Gouge

9. Which is the MOST accurate instrument to use for marking on wood when laying out a joint in cabinet work?

   A. Knife   B. Pencil   C. Scriber   D. Brad awl   E. Nail

10. The fibers running lengthwise in a piece of cloth are called the

    A. heading   B. warp   C. weft   D. nap   E. pile

Questions 11-17.

DIRECTIONS: Questions 11 through 17 refer to the passage that follows. Base your choice on the information given in the selection *and on your own understanding of science.*

The higher forms of plants and animals, such as seed plants and vertebrates, are similar or alike in many respects but decidedly different in others. For example, both of these groups of organisms carry on digestion, respiration, reproduction, conduction, growth, and exhibit sensitivity to various stimuli. On the other hand, a number of basic differences are evident. Plants have no excretory systems comparable to those of animals. Plants have no heart or similar pumping organ. Plants are very limited in their movements. Plants have nothing similar to the animal nervous system. In addition, animals can not synthesize carbohydrates from inorganic substances. Animals do not have special regions of growth, comparable to terminal and lateral meristems in plants, which persist throughout the life span of the organism. And, finally, the animal cell "wall" is only a membrane, while plant cell walls are more rigid, usually thicker, and may be composed of such substances as cellulose, lignin, pectin, cutin, and suberin. These characteristics are important to an understanding of living organisms and their functions and should, consequently, be carefully considered in plant and animal studies.

11. Which of the following do animals lack?

    A. Ability to react to stimuli
    B. Ability to conduct substances from one place to another
    C. Reproduction by gametes
    D. A cell membrane
    E. A terminal growth region

12. Which of the following statements is FALSE?

    A. Animal cell "walls" are composed of cellulose.
    B. Plants grow as long as they live.
    C. Plants produce sperms and eggs.
    D. All vertebrates have hearts.
    E. Wood is dead at maturity.

13. Respiration in plants takes place 13._____

    A. only during the day
    B. only in the presence of carbon dioxide
    C. both day and night
    D. only at night
    E. only in the presence of certain stimuli

14. An example of a vertebrate is the 14._____

    A. earthworm   B. starfish   C. amoeba
    D. cow   E. insect

15. Which of the following statements is TRUE? 15._____

    A. All animals eat plants as a source of food.
    B. Respiration, in many ways, is the reverse of photosynthesis.
    C. Man is an invertebrate animal.
    D. Since plants have no hearts, they can not develop high pressure in their cells.
    E. Plants can not move.

16. Which of the following do plants lack? 16._____

    A. A means of movement   B. Pumping structures
    C. Special regions of growth   D. Reproduction by gametes
    E. A digestive process

17. A substance that can be synthesized by green plants but NOT by animals is 17._____

    A. protein   B. cellulose   C. carbon dioxide
    D. uric acid   E. water

Questions 18-27.

DIRECTIONS: Questions 18 through 27 refer to the passage that follows. Base your choice on the information given in the selection *and on your own understanding of the subject*.

The discovery of antitoxin and its specific antagonistic effect upon toxin furnished an opportunity for the accurate investigation of the relationship of a bacterial antigen and its antibody. Toxin-antitoxin reactions were the first immunological processes to which experimental precision could be applied, and the discovery of principles of great importance resulted from such studies. A great deal of the work was done with diphtheria toxin and antitoxin and the facts elucidated with these materials are in principle applicable to similar substances.

The simplest assumption to account for the manner in which an antitoxin renders a toxin innocuous would be that the antitoxin destroys the toxin. Roux and Buchner, however, advanced the opinion that the antitoxin did not act directly upon the toxin, but affected it indirectly through the mediation of tissue cells. Ehrlich, on the other hand, conceived the reaction of toxin and antitoxin as a direct union, analogous to the chemical neutralization of an acid by a base.

The conception of toxin destruction was conclusively refuted by the experiments of Calmette. This observer, working with snake poison, found that the poison itself (unlike most other toxins) possessed the property of resisting heat to 100 degrees C, while its specific antitoxin, like other antitoxins, was destroyed at or about 70 degrees C. Nontoxic mixtures of the two substances, when subjected to heat, regained their toxic properties. The natural inference from these observations was that the toxin in the original mixture had not been destroyed, but had been merely inactivated by the presence of the antitoxin and again set free after destruction of the antitoxin by heat.

18. Both toxins and antitoxins ordinarily

    A. are completely destroyed at body temperatures
    B. are extremely resistant to heat
    C. can exist only in combination
    D. are destroyed at 180° F
    E. are products of nonliving processes

19. Most toxins can be destroyed by

    A. bacterial action
    B. salt solutions
    C. boiling
    D. diphtheria antitoxin
    E. other toxins

20. Very few disease organisms release a true toxin into the blood stream. It would follow, then, that

    A. studies of snake venom reactions have no value
    B. studies of toxin-antitoxin reactions are of little importance
    C. the treatment of most diseases must depend upon information obtained from study of a few
    D. antitoxin plays an important part in the body defense against the great majority of germs
    E. only toxin producers are dangerous

21. A person becomes susceptible to infection again immediately after recovering from

    A. mumps   B. tetanus   C. diphtheria   D. smallpox
    E. tuberculosis

22. City people are more frequently immune to communicable diseases than country people are because

    A. country people eat better food
    B. city doctors are better than country doctors
    C. the air is more healthful in the country
    D. country people have fewer contacts with disease carriers
    E. there are more doctors in the city than in the country

23. The substance that provide us with immunity to disease are found in the body in the

    A. blood serum   B. gastric juice   C. urine
    D. white blood cells E. red blood cells

24. A person ill with diphtheria would MOST likely be treated with

    A. diphtheria toxin   B. diphtheria toxoid
    C. dead diphtheria germs   D. diphtheria antitoxin
    E. live diphtheria germs

25. To determine susceptibility to diphtheria, an individual may be given the 25.____

    A. Wassermann test   B. Schick test   C. Widal test
    D. Dick test   E. Kahn test

26. Since few babies under six months of age contract diphtheria, young babies PROBABLY 26.____

    A. are never exposed to diphtheria germs
    B. have high body temperatures that destroy the toxin if acquired
    C. acquire immunity from their mothers
    D. acquire immunity from their fathers
    E. are too young to become infected

27. Calmette's findings 27.____

    A. contradicted both Roux and Buchner's opinion and Ehrlich's conception
    B. contradicted Roux and Buchner, but supported Ehrlich
    C. contradicted Ehrlich, but supported Roux and Buchner
    D. were consistent with both theories
    E. had no bearing on the point at issue

Questions 28-37.

DIRECTIONS: Questions 28 through 37 refer to the passage that follows. Base your choice on the information given in the selection *and on your own understanding of the subject.*

Sodium chloride, being by far the largest constituent of the mineral matter of the blood, assumes special significance in the regulation of water exchanges in the organism. And, as Cannon has emphasized repeatedly, these latter are more extensive and more important than may at first thought appear. He points out "there are a number of circulations of the fluid out of the body and back again, without loss." Thus, for example, it is estimated that from a quart to a quart and one-half of water daily "leaves the body" when it enters the mouth as saliva; another one or two quarts are passed out as gastric juice; and perhaps the same amount is contained in the bile and the secretions of the pancreas and the intestinal wall. This large volume of water enters the digestive processes; and practically all of it reabsorbed through the intestinal wall, where it performs the equally important function of carrying in the digested foodstuffs. These and other instances of what Cannon calls "the conservative use of water in our bodies" involve essentially osmotic pressure relationships in which the concentration of sodium chloride plays an important part.

28. This passage implies that 28.____

    A. the contents of the alimentary canal are not to be considered within the body
    B. sodium chloride does not actually enter the body
    C. every particle of water ingested is used over and over again
    D. water can not be absorbed by the body unless it contains sodium chloride
    E. substances can pass through the intestinal wall in only one direction

29. According to this passage, which of the following processes requires MOST water? The

   A. absorption of digested foods
   B. secretion of gastric juice
   C. secretion of saliva
   D. production of bile
   E. concentration of sodium chloride solution

30. A body fluid that is NOT saline is

   A. blood
   B. urine
   C. bile
   D. gastric juice
   E. saliva

31. An organ that functions as a storage reservoir from which large quantities of water are reabsorbed into the body is the

   A. kidney
   B. liver
   C. large intestine
   D. mouth
   E. pancreas

32. Water is reabsorbed into the body by the process of

   A. secretion
   B. excretion
   C. digestion
   D. osmosis
   E. oxidation

33. Digested food enters the body PRINCIPALLY through the

   A. mouth
   B. liver
   C. villi
   D. pancreas
   E. stomach

34. The metallic element found in the blood in compound form and present there in larger quantities than any other metallic element is

   A. iron
   B. calcium
   C. magnesium
   D. chlorine
   E. sodium

35. An organ that removes water from the body and prevents its reabsorption for use in the body processes is the

   A. pancreas
   B. liver
   C. small intestine
   D. lungs
   E. large intestine

36. In which of the following processes is sodium chloride removed MOST rapidly from the body?

   A. Digestion
   B. Breathing
   C. Oxidation
   D. Respiration
   E. Perspiration

37. Which of the following liquids would pass from the alimentary canal into the blood MOST rapidly?

   A. A dilute solution of sodium chloride in water
   B. Gastric juice
   C. A concentrated solution of sodium chloride in water
   D. Digested food
   E. Distilled water

38. The reason why it is unsafe to drink ocean water even under conditions of extreme thirst is that it

   A. would reduce the salinity of the blood to a dangerous level
   B. contains dangerous disease germs
   C. contains poisonous salts

D. would greatly increase the salinity of the blood
E. would cause salt crystals to form in the blood stream

39. When air rises from the surface of the earth, it

    A. contracts and grows warmer
    B. contracts and grows cooler
    C. expands and grows warmer
    D. expands and grows cooler
    E. increases in density

40. The approach of a warm front is USUALLY attended by

    A. cumulus clouds and thunderstorms
    B. stratus clouds and moist air
    C. brisk, northwesterly winds
    D. a rising barometer
    E. clear, dry air

41. A type of air mass that originates in the United States is the

    A. polar continental
    B. polar Atlantic
    C. polar Pacific
    D. tropical gulf
    E. tropical continental

42. The prevailing winds in New York State are

    A. anticyclones
    B. westerlies
    C. trade winds
    D. easterlies
    E. cyclones

43. A meteorologist in New York State would NOT regard as important for weather prediction

    A. the type of clouds in the sky
    B. the weather in Canada, Mexico and Cuba
    C. a change of direction of the wind
    D. a change in the phase of the moon
    E. a change of temperature of the air

44. Which of the following would be of SLIGHT interest to present-day meteorologists?

    A. Winds
    B. Clouds
    C. Precipitation
    D. Fronts
    E. Meteors

45. A cyclonic condition is developing rapidly and is traveling north north-east accompanied by rains and rising temperature. Which of the following important factors was omitted from this report?

    A. Barometric tendency
    B. Precipitation
    C. Storm's path
    D. Temperature tendency
    E. Wind velocity

46. Granite is a rock that was made by

    A. the cementation of sediments
    B. fire in the depths of the earth
    C. the compression of sediments
    D. the cooling of lava deep beneath the earth's surface
    E. the cooling of lava from volcanoes

47. The rate of erosion of cultivated fields with moderate slope can be reduced by

    A. leaving the fields unplanted every other year
    B. planting such crops as corn and potatoes
    C. planting strips of grass up and down the slope
    D. plowing across the slope
    E. planting firm sod around the fields

48. The PRINCIPAL reason for adding agricultural lime to soils is to

    A. improve the texture of the soil
    B. help to preserve the supply of humus
    C. supply materials to stiffen the stems of plants
    D. decrease the acidity of the soil
    E. supply calcium to the growing plants

49. The three elements found MOST commonly in commercial fertilizers are

    A. calcium, phosphorus, iron
    B. nitrogen, phosphorus, potassium
    C. phosphorus, nitrogen, sulfur
    D. calcium, potassium, iron
    E. magnesium, iron, calcium

50. When carbohydrates decompose in the soil, the end products are

    A. nitrates and carbon dioxide
    B. carbon dioxide and water
    C. nitrates and nitrites
    D. carbon monoxide and hydrogen
    E. nitrates and water

KEY (CORRECT ANSWERS)

1. B	11. E	21. E	31. C	41. D
2. B	12. A	22. D	32. D	42. B
3. B	13. C	23. A	33. C	43. D
4. A	14. D	24. D	34. E	44. E
5. B	15. B	25. B	35. D	45. E
6. E	16. B	26. C	36. E	46. D
7. D	17. B	27. D	37. E	47. D
8. D	18. D	28. A	38. D	48. D
9. C	19. C	29. A	39. D	49. B
10. B	20. C	30. D	40. B	50. B

TEST 3

DIRECTIONS: Each question or incomplete statement is followed by several suggested answers or completions. Select the one that BEST answers the question or completes the statement. *PRINT THE LETTER OF THE CORRECT ANSWER IN THE SPACE AT THE RIGHT.*

Questions 1-7.

DIRECTIONS: Questions 1 through 7 refer to the diagram that follows. Base your choice on the information given in the selection and on your own understanding of science.

1. Which of the following is a common insecticide used by gardeners?

    A. Alcohol B. Phosphoric acid C. Wood ashes
    D. Rotenone E. Nitrate of soda

2. The fruit of plants such as the tomato, cucumber, cherry and bean develops from the

    A. receptacle and closely associated stem
    B. petals and closely associated sepals
    C. stem and closely associated parts
    D. ovary and closely associated parts
    E. stamen and closely associated parts

3. The part of the toadstool or mushroom plant that is seen growing above the ground is of PRIMARY use in

    A. reproduction B. transpiration C. food storage
    D. digestion E. photosynthesis

4. Mendel crossed purebred, tall pea plants with dwarf pea plants. The offspring were all tall plants. When he crossed these tall plants with each other, the resulting offsprings were

    A. all tall
    B. about three-fourths tall and one-fourth dwarf
    C. about half tall and half dwarf
    D. about one-fourth tall and three-fourths dwarf
    E. nearly all dwarf

5. A plant cell can BEST be considered a(n)

    A. surface B. volume C. rectangle D. circle E. area

6. The stage in its life cycle in which the clothes moth does MOST harm to woolens is the

    A. blastula B. egg C. larva D. pupa E. adult

7. Lights in chicken houses stimulate egg production by

    A. stimulating in the chickens certain glands that affect formation of egg shells
    B. keeping hens awake so they can lay more eggs
    C. causing hens to consume more food, which results in more eggs produced
    D. increasing the vitamin D content in the hens
    E. controlling the ionization of the air

8. Which of the diseases listed below is caused by animal organism?

   A. Rickets   B. Hay fever   C. Typhoid fever   D. Malaria
   E. Chickenpox

9. Which of the following is a communicable disease?

   A. Scurvy   B. Cancer   C. Goiter
   D. Rabies   E. Nephritis

10. Sulfa drugs are produced CHIEFLY

    A. from a common mold
    B. from glands obtained from animals
    C. by chemical synthesis
    D. by a common bacterium
    E. from the bark of a tree

11. The human body is composed MAINLY of

    A. nitrogen, phosphorus, calcium   B. potassium, nitrogen, oxygen
    C. calcium, iron, potassium   D. carbon, hydrogen, oxygen
    E. iron, calcium, hydrogen

12. The stomach normally contains

    A. some hydrochloric acid   B. some nitric acid
    C. some sulfuric acid   D. some bases but no acids
    E. neither acids nor bases

13. Many of the organic compounds containing nitrogen are called

    A. oils   B. sugars   C. fats   D. starches   E. proteins

14. Man's normal complement of teeth during adulthood is

    A. 24   B. 28   C. 32   D. 36   E. 40

15. Development of the first set of teeth is begun

    A. before birth   B. 12 months after birth
    C. 15 months after birth   D. at birth
    E. 6 months after birth

16. Bacteria enlarge the dentine canals by

    A. eating the walls
    B. allowing the entrance of saliva
    C. stopping the flow of the lymph
    D. movements up and down the canals
    E. producing compounds that attack the walls

17. An experiment was conducted to determine the effect on dental health of introducing a chemical into the drinking water. This chemical contained

    A. magnetium   B. iodine   C. fluorine
    D. calcium   E. iron

18. Rheumatism is sometimes attributed to an abscessed tooth. The abscess may cause the condition by

    A. allowing bacteria to enter the blood
    B. pressing on a nerve
    C. allowing the lymph to escape
    D. producing poisons, which are absorbed
    E. using nutrients that should go to other parts of the body

18.____

19. An enzyme in gastric juice which aids in digesting protein is

    A. ptyalin   B. trypsin   C. amylopsin   D. pepsin
    E. maltase

19.____

20. To help prevent scarlet fever from spreading from one member of a household to other members, it is MOST essential to

    A. get a trained nurse
    B. keep the room temperature at 72° F
    C. have attendants change outer clothing upon leaving the sickroom
    D. remove all unnecessary accessories from the sickroom
    E. keep the patient in a warm room with windows closed

20.____

21. Of the following possible effects of an automobile accident, the condition that requires MOST immediate treatment is

    A. spinal dislocation   B. shock
    C. concussion   D. tetanus
    E. arterial bleeding

21.____

22. When rags used by painters to wipe up linseed oil catch fire spontaneously, it is because

    A. paint oil gives off oxygen readily
    B. paint oil oxidizes
    C. the cloth reduces the oxygen in the paint oil
    D. the paint oil reduces the oxygen in the cloth
    E. paint oil and cloth unite chemically

22.____

23. Alum is added to water in many municipal water systems to

    A. reduce unwanted dissolved gases
    B. remove objectionable flavors
    C. kill harmful bacteria
    D. soften the water
    E. remove sediment

23.____

24. Soap aids in cleaning because its action on greases and oils is to

    A. reduce them   B. oxidize them   C. emulsify them
    D. dissolve them   E. precipitate them

24.____

25. When a candle burns, the CHIEF products are

    A. carbon dioxide and carbon monoxide
    B. carbon dioxide and nitrogen
    C. carbon monoxide and nitrogen

25.____

D. carbon monoxide and water
E. carbon dioxide and water

26. Iron is removed from its oxide ores by

    A. roasting the ore
    B. reducing the ore with carbon
    C. oxidizing the ore with a blast of air
    D. melting the ore, thus allowing the iron to escape
    E. making a slag to absorb the oxides of the iron

27. A mineral much used as a source of iron is

    A. galena   B. hematite   C. franklinite   D. chromite
    E. halite

28. A gas generally used in incandescent lamps to increase their operating efficiency is

    A. freon   B. oxygen   C. neon   D. argon   E. chlorine

29. The meter whose readings are used in determining the amount of the monthly household electric bill measures

    A. voltage   B. electrical energy   C. power
    D. amperage   E. electrical resistance

30. Most household appliances using electric motors are made to operate on

    A. 110-volt alternating current   B. 110-volt direct current
    C. 32-volt direct current   D. 6-volt direct current
    E. 1 1/2-volt direct current

31. A bimetallic thermostat operates because

    A. metals expand when heated
    B. different metals expand at different rates when heated
    C. two metals will conduct electric currents at different rates
    D. a voltage is produced between the junctions of the two metals when one junction is heated
    E. different metals appear on different levels in the electromotive series

32. A transformer is used to change

    A. alternating current to direct current
    B. the voltage of alternating current
    C. the voltage of direct current
    D. the frequency of alternating current
    E. direct current to alternating current

33. One material much used for permanent magnets is

    A. steel   B. soft iron   C. copper   D. zinc   E. carbon

5 (#3)

34. The surfaces of a thermos bottle are silvered to

   A. reduce convection
   B. reduce radiation
   C. reduce conduction
   D. keep out ultraviolet rays
   E. make cleaning easier

35. A temperature of 25° C is NEAREST to which of the following temperatures?

   A. 20° F   B. 40° F   C. 60° F   D. 80° F   E. 100° F

36. Ice floats because

   A. water becomes denser as it cools
   B. it contains so much air
   C. water expands when it freezes
   D. fish could not live in ponds if the ice sank to the bottom
   E. water expands as it cools from 4° C to 0° C

37. If a person facing a high cliff hears his echo 5 seconds after he shouts, the distance between the person and the cliff is about

   A. 1/4 mile   B. 1/2 mile   C. 3/4 mile
   D. 1 mile   E. 1 1/4 miles

38. The horizontal stabilizers of a plane are necessary to

   A. make the plane dive and climb
   B. make the plane bank on a turn
   C. keep the tail from bobbing up and down
   D. enable the pilot to turn right or left
   E. keep the plane from weaving from side to side

39. A good quality lumber for outside woodwork is

   A. basswood   B. hard maple   C. yellow birch
   D. white pine   E. red gumwood

40. Knots in lumber are caused by

   A. boring insects   B. branches   C. winter injury
   D. decay   E. unequal growth

41. On which of the following woods MUST a paste filler be used during the finishing process?

   A. Basswood   B. Maple   C. Oak   D. Redgum   E. Cedar

42. In what order should the dimension of boards be listed when ordering lumber from a mill?

   A. Length, width, thickness
   B. Thickness, width, length
   C. Length, thickness, width
   D. Width, length, thickness
   E. Width, thickness, length

43. The number of a wood screw indicates its

   A. number of threads per inch
   B. style of point
   C. length
   D. style of head
   E. diameter

44. Half-and-half solder is an alloy composed of

   A. lead and tin
   B. tin and copper
   C. tin and zinc
   D. lead and brass
   E. zinc and lead

45. The process used to make earthenware waterproof is known as

   A. glazing   B. finishing   C. molding   D. firing
   E. decorating

46. Molds for casting clay are made of

   A. plaster of paris   B. galvanized iron   C. tin
   D. wood   E. cardboard

47. A tool used to cut the thread in a nut is a

   A. tap   B. die   C. reamer   D. drill   E. bolt

48. To draw vertical lines in drafting, one should use

   A. a T square   B. a rule   C. a triangle
   D. two triangles   E. a T square and triangle

49. The pica is a unit of measurement in

   A. ceramics   B. printing   C. toolmaking
   D. photography   E. textile design

50. Of the following, the fiber that is MOST weakened by being wet is

   A. cotton   B. rayon   C. linen   D. silk   E. wool

KEY (CORRECT ANSWERS)

1. D	11. D	21. E	31. B	41. C
2. D	12. A	22. B	32. B	42. B
3. A	13. E	23. E	33. A	43. E
4. B	14. C	24. C	34. B	44. A
5. B	15. A	25. E	35. D	45. A
6. C	16. E	26. B	36. C	46. A
7. A	17. C	27. B	37. B	47. A
8. D	18. D	28. D	38. C	48. E
9. D	19. D	29. B	39. D	49. B
10. C	20. C	30. A	40. B	50. E

TEST 4

DIRECTIONS: Each question or incomplete statement is followed by several suggested answers or completions. Select the one that BEST answers the question or completes the statement. *PRINT THE LETTER OF THE CORRECT ANSWER IN THE SPACE AT THE RIGHT.*

Questions 1-7.

DIRECTIONS: Questions 1 through 7 refer to the diagram that follows. Base your choice on the information given in the selection and on your own understanding of science.

1. The revolving part of an automobile generator is the

    A. cam   B. slipring   C. armature
    D. coil   E. brushes

2. A by-product of soap manufacture is

    A. acetone   B. benzine   C. fat   D. glycerin   E. lye

3. When a certain quantity of water is decomposed by electrolysis, 60 cubic centimeters of hydrogen are produced. The number of cubic centimeters of oxygen obtained is

    A. 20   B. 30   C. 60   D. 120   E. 180

4. Of the following, the BEST conductor of heat is

    A. asbestos   B. brass   C. copper   D. glass   E. iron

5. The temperature of the air falls during the night, PRINCIPALLY because the earth loses heat by

    A. conduction   B. convection   C. insolation   D. radiation
    E. reflection

6. The relative humidity of the air when dew forms is

    A. 10%   B. 25%   C. 50%   D. 75%   E. 100%

7. The low-pressure areas that bring stormy weather to New York State USUALLY come from the

    A. east   B. north   C. south   D. southeast   E. west

8. An instrument used to determine latitude is the

    A. altimeter   B. barometer   C. isobar   D. hydrometer
    E. sextant

9. The earth rotates 30 degrees in

    A. 1 hour   B. 2 hours   C. 3 hours   D. 4 hours   E. 5 hours

10. The earth is NEAREST the sun in the month of

    A. January   B. March   C. June   D. September   E. December

11. All parts of the earth have 12 hours of daylight on

   A. December 21st   B. June 21st   C. July 21st
   D. March 21st   E. November 21st

12. Eastern Double Daylight Saving Time corresponds to the standard time at the meridian of west longitude numbered

   A. 60   B. 75   C. 90   D. 105   E. 120

13. We see one-half of the lighted portion of the moon at the

   A. first quarter   B. full moon   C. new crescent
   D. new moon   E. old crescent

14. A planet whose orbit is between the sun and the orbit of the earth is

   A. Jupiter   B. Mars   C. Pluto   D. Saturn   E. Venus

15. The changing position of the stars during the night is MAINLY the result of the

   A. inclination of the earth's axis
   B. rotation of the earth
   C. rotation of the stars
   D. revolution of the earth
   E. revolution of the stars

16. The gravational force of the moon is exerted

   A. only upon the side of the earth nearest the moon
   B. only upon the point on the earth nearest the moon
   C. upon the center of the earth only
   D. upon the entire earth
   E. upon the water surfaces of the earth but not upon the land surfaces

17. The work done by tides is gradually slowing down the earth's period of rotation. It is, therefore, reasonable to predict that, millions of years from now,

   A. the earth will be farther away from the moon than now
   B. the frequency of tides will be greater than now
   C. days will be shorter than they are now
   D. phases of the moon will change more rapidly than now
   E. lunar months will be longer than they are now

18. The earth's gravitational attraction is GREATEST at

   A. the North Pole
   B. the equator
   C. a point on the earth's surface directly under the moon
   D. a point on the earth's surface exactly opposite the moon
   E. a point 10 miles above the earth's surface, whatever the position of the moon

19. The part of the seed that develops into the young plant is called the

   A. cotyledon   B. embryo   C. hilum
   D. micropyle   E. testa

20. The union of the sperm and the egg cells of flowers is called   20._____

    A. fertilization   B. maturation   C. parthenogenesis
    D. pollination   E. sporulation

21. An insect that eats no food during the adult stage is the   21._____

    A. grasshopper   B. bumblebee   C. cricket
    D. Japanese beetle   E. Cecropia moth

22. The image of an object is formed in the eye on the   22._____

    A. cornea   B. pupil   C. iris   D. lens   E. retina

23. An organ located above the diaphragm is the   23._____

    A. stomach   B. liver   C. heart   D. pancreas   E. spleen

24. Of the following, an organ that is NOT connected with the alimentary canal is the   24._____

    A. pancreas   B. liver   C. kidney   D. salivary glands
    E. appendix

25. The ptyalin in saliva is a(n)   25._____

    A. auxin   B. chalone   C. enzyme   D. hormone   E. vitamin

26. Glucose is stored in the liver and muscles in the form of   26._____

    A. glycogen   B. levulose   C. glycocoll   D. fat   E. dextrose

27. A substance that is readily absorbed through the walls of the stomach is   27._____

    A. starch   B. sugar   C. alcohol   D. amino acids
    E. ascorbic acid

28. The poisonouc character of carbon monoxide is due to its tendency to unite chemically   28._____
    with

    A. water   B. synovial fluid   C. cerebrospinal fluid
    D. hemoglobin   E. gastric juice

29. A nutrient that contains nitrogen is   29._____

    A. fat   B. protein   C. starch   D. sugar   E. water

30. A substance that is a carbohydrate is   30._____

    A. glutenin   B. stearin   C. palmitin
    D. gliadin   E. dextrin

31. A food that contains no vitamins is   31._____

    A. white potato   B. cane sugar   C. dried beans
    D. lard   E. white bread

32. Of the following, the vegetable that contains the HIGHEST percentage of protein is the   32._____

    A. tomato   B. cabbage   C. carrot
    D. lima bean   E. head lettuce

33. When bread is toasted, much of the starch is changed to

   A. dextrose   B. maltose   C. maltase   D. dextrin   E. biotin

34. A preparation of dead or weakened bacilli used for developing immunity to a disease is called a(n)

   A. vaccine   B. virus   C. culture medium   D. antitoxin
   E. immune serum

35. A disease caused by a virus is

   A. anthrax   B. dysentery   C. scurvy   D. smallpox
   E. tuberculosis

36. Of the following diseases, the one that is NOT caused by a filtrable virus is

   A. syphilis   B. yellow fever   C. measles   D. mumps
   E. infantile paralysis

37. A disease that may be prevented by the use of a vaccine is

   A. tuberculosis   B. poliomyelitis   C. rabies
   D. gonorrhea   E. dementia praecox

38. Immunity to diphtheria may be detected by the use of

   A. the Dick test   B. the Schick test
   C. arsphenamine   D. acetylsalicylate
   E. the Wassermann test

39. A substance used to treat malaria is

   A. sodium perborate   B. atabrine   C. penicillin
   D. salol   E. sulfathiazole

40. Silicosis may result from prolonged exposure to

   A. radium   B. poisonous gases   C. ragweed pollen
   D. metallic dusts   E. rock dusts

41. Trichinosis is a disease contracted MOSTLY from

   A. chicken   B. beef   C. pork   D. lamb   E. fish

42. Delay in the removal of an inflamed appendix sometimes results in

   A. peritonitis   B. gingivitis   C. gastritis
   D. phlebitis   E. meningitis

43. Blowing the nose hard during a cold is dangerous, PRIMARILY because the

   A. back pressure may force bacteria into the eustachian tubes
   B. lining of the nose may be damaged
   C. lungs may be overworked
   D. flow of mucus may be stopped
   E. nasal sinuses may burst

44. Mouth washes

    A. kill whatever germs are present in the mouth
    B. are effective in preventing diseases
    C. prevent germs from entering the mouth
    D. prevent the growth of germs in the mouth
    E. are of little or no health value

45. Dissolved impurities can be separated from water by

    A. aeration   B. chlorination   C. distillation
    D. filtration   E. settling

46. Lake or river water may be made safe to drink by letting the water stand one-half hour after adding

    A. two drops of tincture of iodine per quart
    B. one pint of ethyl alcohol per gallon
    C. one drop of sulfuric acid per quart
    D. 10 grams of table salt per gallon
    E. one aspirin tablet per pint

47. A dermatologist is a physician who specializes in the care of

    A. children   B. the hair   C. the skin   D. old people
    E. chronic diseases

48. Schizophrenia is a

    A. dangerous drug
    B. mental disorder
    C. dye used in staining tissue cells
    D. communicable disease
    E. hormone

49. An example of rationalization is

    A. building up an exaggerated tendency that is opposite to the unconscious wish
    B. justifying failure by means of arguments that excuse it
    C. complete forgetting of unfavorable experiences
    D. identifying oneself with a hero of some sort
    E. gratifying wishes by assuming an illness

50. The nutrient provided by milk and milk products that is MOST difficult to obtain from other common foods is

    A. vitamin A   B. calcium   C. complete protein
    D. niacin   E. vitamin C

KEY (CORRECT ANSWERS)

1. C	11. D	21. E	31. B	41. C
2. D	12. A	22. E	32. D	42. A
3. B	13. A	23. C	33. D	43. A
4. C	14. E	24. C	34. A	44. E
5. D	15. B	25. C	35. D	45. C
6. E	16. D	26. A	36. A	46. A
7. E	17. A	27. C	37. C	47. C
8. E	18. A	28. D	38. B	48. B
9. B	19. B	29. B	39. B	49. B
10. A	20. A	30. E	40. E	50. B

TEST 5

DIRECTIONS: Each question or incomplete statement is followed by several suggested answers or completions. Select the one that BEST answers the question or completes the statement. *PRINT THE LETTER OF THE CORRECT ANSWER IN THE SPACE AT THE RIGHT.*

Questions 1-7.

DIRECTIONS: Questions 1 through 7 refer to the passage that follows. Base your choice on the information in the passage *and on your own knowledge of science.*

In the days of sailing ships, when voyages were long and uncertain, provisions for many months were stored without refrigeration in the holds of the ships. Naturally no fresh or perishable foods could be included. Toward the end of particularly long voyages the crews of such ships became ill and often many died from scurvy. Many men, both scientific and otherwise, tried to devise a cure for scurvy. Among the latter was John Hall, a son-in-law of William Shakespeare, who cured some cases of scurvy by administering a sour brew made from scurvy grass and watercress.

The next step was the suggestion of William Harvey that scurvy could be prevented by giving the men lemon juice. He thought that the beneficial substance was the acid contained in the fruit.

The third step was taken by Dr. James Lind, an English naval surgeon, who performed the following experiment with 12 sailors all of whom were sick with scurvy: Each was given the same diet, except that four of the men received small amounts of dilute sulfuric acid, four others were given vinegar and the remaining four were given lemons. Only those who received the fruit recovered.

1. Credit for solving the problem described above belongs to

   A. HALL, because he first devised a cure for scurvy
   B. HARVEY, because he first proposed a solution of the problem
   C. LIND, because he proved the solution by means of an experiment
   D. both HARVEY and LIND, because they found that lemons are more effective than scurvy grass or watercress
   E. all three men, because each made some contribution

2. A good substitute for lemons in the treatment of scurvy is

   A. fresh eggs   B. tomato juice   C. cod-liver oil
   D. liver   E. whole-wheat bread

3. The number of control groups that Dr. Lind used in his experiment was

   A. one   B. two   C. three   D. four   E. none

4. A substance that will turn blue litmus red is

   A. aniline   B. lye   C. ice   D. vinegar   E. table salt

5. The hypothesis tested by Lind was:

   A. Lemons contain some substance not present in vinegar.
   B. Citric acid is the most effective treatment for scurvy.
   C. Lemons contain some unknown acid that will cure scurvy.
   D. Some specific substance, rather than acids in general, is needed to cure scurvy.
   E. The substance needed to cure scurvy is found only in lemons.

6. A problem that Lind's experiment did NOT solve was:

   A. Will citric acid alone cure scurvy?
   B. Will lemons cure scurvy?
   C. Will either sulfuric acid or vinegar cure scurvy?
   D. Are all substances that contain acids equally effective as a treatment for scurvy?
   E. Are lemons more effective than either vinegar or sulfuric acid in the treatment of scurvy?

7. The PRIMARY purpose of a controlled scientific experiment is to

   A. get rid of superstitions
   B. prove a hypothesis is correct
   C. disprove a theory that is false
   D. determine whether a hypothesis is true or false
   E. discover new facts

Questions 8-15.

DIRECTIONS: Questions 8 through 15 refer to the passage that follows. Base your choice on the information in the passage and *on your own knowledge of science*.

Photosynthesis is a complex process with many intermediate steps. Ideas differ greatly as to the details of these steps, but the general nature of the process and its outcome are well established. Water, usually from the soil, is conducted through the xylem of root, stem and leaf to the chlorophyl-containing cells of a leaf. In consequence of the abundance of water within the latter cells, their walls are saturated with water. Carbon dioxide, diffusing from the air through the stomata and into the intercellular spaces of the leaf, comes into contact with the water in the walls of the cells, which adjoin the intercellular spaces. The carbon dioxide becomes dissolved in the water in these walls, and in solution diffuses through the walls and the plasma membranes into the cells. By the agency of chlorphyl in the chloroplasts of the cells, the energy of light is transformed into chemical energy. This chemical energy is used to decompose the carbon dioxide and water, and the products of their decomposition are recombined into a new compound. The compound first formed is successively built up into more and more complex substances until finally a sugar is produced.

8. The union of carbon dioxide and water to form starch results in an excess of

   A. hydrogen   B. carbon   C. oxygen
   D. carbon monoxide   E. hydrogen peroxide

9. Synthesis of carbohydrates takes place

   A. in the stomata
   B. in the intercellular spaces of leaves
   C. in the walls of plant cells
   D. within the plasma membranes of plant cells
   E. within plant cells that contain chloroplasts

10. In the process of photosynthesis, chlorophyl acts as a   10.____

    A. carbohydrate
    B. source of carbon dioxide
    C. catalyst
    D. source of chemical energy
    E. plasma membrane

11. In which of the following places are there the GREATEST number of hours in which photosynthesis can take place during the month of December?   11.____

    A. Buenos Aires, Argentina
    B. Caracas, Venezuela
    C. Fairbanks, Alaska
    D. Quito, Ecuador
    E. Calcutta, India

12. During photosynthesis, molecules of carbon dioxide enter the stomata of leaves because   12.____

    A. the molecules are already in motion
    B. they are forced through the stomata by the sun's rays
    C. chlorophyl attracts them
    D. a chemical change takes place in the stomata
    E. oxygen passes out through the stomata

13. Besides food manufacture, another useful result of photosynthesis is that it   13.____

    A. aids in removing poisonous gases from the air
    B. helps to maintain the existing proportion of gases in the air
    C. changes complex compounds into simpler compounds
    D. changes certain waste products into hydrocarbons
    E. changes chlorophyl into useful substances

14. A process that is ALMOST the exact reverse of photosynthesis is the   14.____

    A. rusting of iron
    B. burning of wood
    C. digestion of starch
    D. ripening of fruit
    E. storage of food in seeds

15. The leaf of the tomato plant will be unable to carry on photosynthesis if the   15.____

    A. upper surface of the leaf is coated with vaseline
    B. upper surface of the leaf is coated with lampblack
    C. lower surface of the leaf is coated with lard
    D. leaf is placed in an atmosphere of pure carbon dioxide
    E. entire leaf is coated with lime

Questions 16-24.

DIRECTIONS: Questions 16 through 24 refer to the passage that follows. Base your choice on the information in the passage and *on your own knowledge of science*.

The British pressure suit was made in two pieces and joined around the middle in contrast to the other suits, which were one-piece suits with a removable helmet. Oxygen was supplied through a tube, and a container of soda lime absorbed carbon dioxide and water vapor. The pressure was adjusted to a maximum of 2 1/2 pounds per square inch (130 millimeters) higher than the surrounding air. Since pure oxygen was used, this produced a partial pressure of 130 millimeters, which is sufficient to sustain the flier at any altitude.

Using this pressure suit, the British established a world's altitude record of 49,944 feet in 1936 and succeeded in raising it to 53,937 feet the following year. The pressure suit is a compromise solution to the altitude problem. Full sea-level pressure cannot be maintained, as the suit would be so rigid that the flier could not move arms or legs. Hence a pressure one-third to one-fifth that of sea level has been used. Because of these lower pressures, oxygen has been used to raise the partial pressure of alveolar oxygen to normal.

16. The MAIN constituent of air NOT admitted to the pressure suit described was

    A. oxygen   B. nitrogen   C. water vapor
    D. carbon dioxide   E. hydrogen

17. The pressure within the suit exceeded that of the surrounding air by an amount equal to 130 millimeters of

    A. mercury   B. water   C. air
    D. oxygen   E. carbon dioxide

18. The normal atmospheric pressure at sea level is

    A. 130 mm   B. 250 mm   C. 760 mm   D. 1000 mm   E. 1300 mm

19. The water vapor that was absorbed by the soda lime came from

    A. condensation
    B. the union of oxygen with carbon dioxide
    C. body metabolism
    D. the air within the pressure suit
    E. water particles in the upper air

20. The HIGHEST altitude that has been reached with the British pressure suit is about

    A. 130 miles   B. 2 1/2 miles   C. 6 miles   D. 10 miles
    E. 5 miles

21. If the pressure suit should develop a leak, the

    A. oxygen supply would be cut off
    B. suit would fill up with air instead of oxygen
    C. pressure within the suit would drop to zero
    D. pressure within the suit would drop to that of the surrounding air
    E. suit would become so rigid that the flier would be unable to move arms or legs

22. The reason why oxygen helmets are unsatisfactory for use in efforts to set higher altitude records is that

    A. it is impossible to maintain a tight enough fit at the neck
    B. oxygen helmets are too heavy
    C. they do not conserve the heat of the body as pressure suits do

5 (#5)

    D. if a parachute jump becomes necessary, it cannot be made while such a helmet is being worn
    E. oxygen helmets are too rigid

23. The pressure suit is termed a compromise solution because   23.____

    A. it is not adequate for stratosphere flying
    B. aviators cannot stand sea-level pressure at high altitudes
    C. some suits are made in two pieces, others in one
    D. other factors than maintenance of pressure have to be accommodated
    E. full atmospheric pressure cannot be maintained at high altitudes

24. The passage implies that   24.____

    A. the air pressure at 49,944 feet is approximately the same as it is at 53,937 feet
    B. pressure cabin planes are not practical at extremely high altitudes
    C. a flier's oxygen requirement is approximately the same at high altitudes as it is at sea level
    D. one-piece pressure suits with removable helmets are unsafe
    E. a normal alveolar oxygen supply is maintained if the air pressure is between one-third and one-fifth that of sea level

25. If two 100-lb forces act concurrently so that their resultant is 50 lbs., the angle between them is which one of the following?   25.____

    A. Acute   B. Right   C. Obtuse   D. Straight   E. Oblique

26. The frequency of vibration of a string varies   26.____

    A. directly as the length
    B. directly as the square root of the tension
    C. inversely as the weight per unit length
    D. directly as the square root of the length
    E. directly as the length and inversely as the square foot of the tension

27. A 40 lb. force acting at an angle of $30°$ with a lever produces the same moment as a second force applied perpendicularly at the same point. The magnitude of this second force (in pounds) is   27.____

    A. 20   B. 35   C. 60   D. 80   E. 100

28. Assume that a simple pendulum has a period of one second. If the mass of the bob is doubled, and the length of the string is quadrupled, the new period (in seconds) is   28.____

    A. one   B. two   C. four   D. eight   E. sixteen

29. A given mass of an ideal gas is heated isothermally until it has a volume of 200 cm . If initially the gas had a volume of 100 cm^3 at a gauge pressure of 15 lb/in^2 , the final guage pressure (in pounds per square inch) will be CLOSEST to which one of the following?   29.____

    A. zero   B. 7.5   C. 15   D. 30   E. 60

30. A pulley with a mechanical advantage of two is used to lift a 500 lb. weight 20 ft. The potential energy of the weight (in ft.lb) increased

   A. 500   B. 5,000   C. 10,000   D. 20,000   E. 40,000

31. Of the following, the natural process which might require an energy input of about 10^{24} ergs/hour is

   A. the glow of a firefly
   B. a hurricane
   C. a bird's flight
   D. insolation per square foot at the equator
   E. an earthquake

32. If the molecules in a cylinder of oxygen and those in a cylinder of hydrogen have the same average speed, then

   A. both gases have the same temperature
   B. both gases have the same pressure
   C. the hydrogen has the higher temperature
   D. the oxygen has the higher temperature
   E. the hydrogen has the higher temperature when the oxygen has the lower temperature

33. Of the following, which condition exists in a perfectly inelastic collision?

   A. Neither momentum nor kinetic energy are conserved
   B. Both momentum and kinetic energy are conserved
   C. Momentum is conserved, but not kinetic energy
   D. Kinetic energy is conserved, but not momentum
   E. There is no relationship between momentum and kinetic energy

34. A simple series circuit consists of a cell, an ammeter, and a rheostat of resistance R. The ammeter reads 5 amps. When the resistance of the rheostat is increased by 2 ohms, the ammeter reading drops to 4 amps. The original resistance (in ohms) of the rheostat R is

   A. 2.5   B. 4.0   C. 8.0   D. 10.0   E. 12.0

35. A simple steam engine receives steam from the boiler at 180° C and exhausts directly into the air at 100° C. The upper limit of its thermal efficiency (in percent) is CLOSEST to which one of the following?

   A. 17.6   B. 28.0   C. 35.5   D. 80.0   E. 92.6

36. Two lamps need 50V and 2 amp each in order to operate at a desired brilliancy. If they are to be connected in series across a 120V line, the resistance (in ohms) of the rheostat that must be placed in series with the lamps needs to be

   A. 4   B. 10   C. 20   D. 100   E. 200

37. As the photon is a quantum in electromagnetic field theory, which one of the following is considered to be the quantum in the nuclear field?

   A. Neutrino   B. Electron   C. Meson   D. Neutron
   E. None of them

38. A 5 diopter lens has a focal length (in cm) CLOSEST to which one of the following?

    A. 1/5   B. 5   C. 20   D. 50   E. 100

39. The infra-red spectrometer has a prism that is GENERALLY made of which one of the following?

    A. Quartz
    B. Glass
    C. Sodium chloride
    D. Carbon disulfide
    E. Sodium disulfide

40. When an electron moves with a speed equal to 4/5 that of light, the ratio of its mass to its rest mass is which one of the following?

    A. 5/4   B. 5/3   C. 25/9   D. 25/16   E. 4/5

41. A pulley on an electric motor turns clockwise. A crossed belt turns a much larger pulley on a feed grinder. The pulley on the feed grinder turns

    A. clockwise and slower than the one on the motor
    B. counterclockwise and slower than the one on the motor
    C. clockwise and faster than the one on the motor
    D. counterclockwise and faster than the one on the motor
    E. clockwise and at the same speed as the one on the motor

42. The sprocket wheels and chain of a bicycle increase the

    A. power of the rider
    B. force applied to the rear wheel
    C. force applied to the road
    D. speed of the rear wheel
    E. energy output of the rider

43. Soda pop rises along a soda straw into one's mouth because

    A. nature abhors a vacuum
    B. there is capillary action in the straw
    C. the air pressure on the pop is greater than the pressure in one's mouth
    D. the vacuum in one's mouth pulls up the pop
    E. the carbon dioxide pressure in the pop forces it upwards

44. Which of the following principles BEST explains the propulsion of a jet plane?

    A. Every action has an equal and opposite reaction
    B. Energy can be neither created nor destroyed
    C. Every effect has a cause
    D. If pressure is applied to a confined gas, the volume of the gas will decrease
    E. Compression of a gas produces heat

45. To make an airplane bank on a left turn, the left

    A. elevator is raised and the right elevator is lowered
    B. pedal is pushed and the right pedal is pulled
    C. aileron is raised and the right aileron is lowered
    D. stabilizer is raised and the right stabilizer is lowered
    E. wing is tilted upward and the right wing is tilted downward

46. A ship entering a fresh-water river from the ocean will sink deeper because

   A. salt water has greater viscosity than fresh water
   B. salt holds objects up
   C. a cubic foot of salt water weighs more than a cubic foot of fresh water
   D. surface tension is greater in the river
   E. oceans are deeper

47. The fuel in the cylinder of a Diesel engine is ignited by

   A. an electric spark   B. a pilot light   C. the injector
   D. a supercharger   E. the heat of compression

48. A three-element vacuum tube in an electric circuit

   A. generates signals of increased voltage
   B. amplifies the grid bias
   C. controls the electron flow in the circuit
   D. rectifies the B-battery output
   E. increases the signal frequency

49. Some highways are lighted at night by lamps that produce a golden-yellow light. This color is due to the passage of electricity through the vapor of

   A. argon   B. helium   C. mercury   D. nitrogen   E. sodium

50. A fluorescent lamp produces light by the

   A. ionization of the Heaviside layer
   B. glowing of an incandescent filament
   C. production of X-rays
   D. action of infrared rays, which heat the glass
   E. action of ultraviolet rays on a mineral coating on the glass

---

KEY (CORRECT ANSWERS)

1. E	11. A	21. D	31. B	41. B
2. B	12. A	22. D	32. D	42. D
3. B	13. B	23. E	33. C	43. C
4. D	14. B	24. C	34. C	44. A
5. D	15. C	25. C	35. A	45. C
6. A	16. B	26. B	36. B	46. C
7. D	17. A	27. A	37. C	47. E
8. C	18. C	28. B	38. C	48. C
9. E	19. C	29. A	39. C	49. E
10. C	20. D	30. C	40. B	50. E

READING COMPREHENSION
UNDERSTANDING AND INTERPRETING WRITTEN MATERIAL
EXAMINATION SECTION
TEST 1

DIRECTIONS: Each question or incomplete statement is followed by several suggested answers or completions. Select the one that BEST answers the question or completes the statement. *PRINT THE LETTER OF THE CORRECT ANSWER IN THE SPACE AT THE RIGHT.*

Questions 1-4.

DIRECTIONS: Questions 1 through 4 are to be answered SOLELY on the basis of the following paragraph.

Rodent control must be planned carefully in order to insure its success. This means that more knowledge is needed about the habits and favorite breeding places of Domestic Rats than any other kind. A favorite breeding place for Domestic Rats is known to be in old or badly constructed buildings. Rats find these buildings very comfortable for making nests. However, the only way to gain this kind of detailed knowledge about rats is through careful study.

1. According to the above paragraph, rats find comfortable nesting places   1.____

    A. in old buildings   B. in pipes
    C. on roofs   D. in sewers

2. The paragraph states that the BEST way to learn all about the favorite nesting places of rats is by   2.____

    A. asking people   B. careful study
    C. using traps   D. watching ratholes

3. According to the paragraph, in order to insure the success of rodent control, it is necessary to   3.____

    A. design better bait   B. give out more information
    C. plan carefully   D. use pesticides

4. The paragraph states that the MOST important rats to study are _____ Rats.   4.____

    A. African   B. Asian   C. Domestic   D. European

Questions 5-8.

DIRECTIONS: Questions 5 through 8 are to be answered SOLELY on the basis of the following paragraph.

People are very suspicious of all strangers who knock at their door. For this reason, every pest control aide, whether man or woman, must carry an identification card at all times on the job. These cards are issued by the agency the aide works for. The aide's picture is on the card. The aide's name is typed in, and the aide's signature is written on the line below.

The name, address, and telephone number of the agency issuing the card is also printed on it. Once the aide shows this ID card to prove his or her identity, the tenant's time should not be taken up with small talk. The tenant should be told briefly what pest control means. The aide should be polite and ready to answer any questions the tenant may have on the subject. Then, the aide should thank the tenant for listening and say goodbye.

5. According to the above paragraph, when she visits tenants, the one item a pest control aide must ALWAYS carry with her is a(n)

   A. badge
   B. driver's license
   C. identification card
   D. watch

6. According to the paragraph, a pest control aide is supposed to talk to each tenant he visits

   A. at length about the agency
   B. briefly about pest control
   C. at length about family matters
   D. briefly about social security

7. According to the paragraph, the item that does NOT appear on an ID card is the

   A. address of the agency
   B. name of the agency
   C. signature of the aide
   D. social security number of the aide

8. According to the paragraph, a pest control aide carries an identification card because he must

   A. prove to tenants who he is
   B. provide the tenant with the agency's address
   C. provide the tenant with the agency's telephone number
   D. save the tenant's time

Questions 9-12.

DIRECTIONS: Questions 9 through 12 are to be answered SOLELY on the basis of the following paragraphs.

The insects you, as a Housing Exterminator, will control are just a minute fraction of the millions which inhabit the world. Man does well to hold his own in the face of the constant pressures that insects continue to exert upon him. Not only are the total numbers tremendous, but the number of individual kinds, or species, certainly exceeds 800,000 — a number greater than that of all other animals combined. Many of these are beneficial, but some are especially competitive with man. Not only are insects numerous, but they are among the most adaptable of all animals. In their many forms, they are fitted for almost any specific way of life. Their adaptability, combined with their tremendous rate of reproduction, gives insects an unequaled potential for survival

The food of insects includes almost anything that can be eaten by any other animal, as well as many things which cannot even be digested by any other animals. Most insects do not harm the products of man or carry diseases harmful to him; however, many do carry diseases, and others feed on his food and manufactured goods. Some are adapted to living only in open areas, while others are able to live in extremely confined spaces. All of these factors combined make the insects a group of animals having many members which are a nuisance to man and thus of great importance to the Housing Exterminator.

The control of insects requires an understanding of their way of life. Thus, it is necessary for the Housing Exterminator to understand the anatomy of the insect, its method of growth, the time it takes for the insect to grow from egg to adult, its habits, the stage of its life history in which it causes damage, its food, and its common living places. In order to obtain the best control, it is especially important to be able to identify correctly the specific insect involved because without this knowledge, it is impossible to prescribe a proper treatment.

9. Which one of the following is a CORRECT statement about the insect population of the world according to the above paragraph?
The

   A. total number of insects is less than the total number of all other animals combined
   B. number of species of insects is greater than the number of species of all other animals combined
   C. total number of harmful insects is greater than the total number of those which are not harmful
   D. number of species of harmless insects is less than the number of species of those which are harmful

10. Insects will be controlled MOST efficiently if the Housing Exterminator

   A. understands why the insects are so numerous
   B. knows what insects he is dealing with
   C. sees if the insects compete with man
   D. is able to identify the food which the insects digest

11. According to the above passage, insects are of importance to an exterminator PRIMARILY because they

   A. can be annoying, destructive, and harmful to man
   B. are able to thrive in very small spaces
   C. cause damage during their growth stages
   D. are so adaptable that they can adjust to any environment

12. According to the above passage, insects can eat

   A. everything that any other living thing can eat
   B. man's food and things which he makes
   C. anything which other animals can't digest
   D. only food and food products

Questions 13-22.

DIRECTIONS: Questions 13 through 22 are to be answered SOLELY on the basis of the following instructions.

INSTRUCTIONS FOR PREPARATION AND PLACEMENT OF RAT BAITS

1. Fresh baits are the most acceptable to rats, so mix only enough bait for current needs. Use a binder of molasses or of vegetable, mineral or fish oil in cereal or dry baits to hold the poison and the dry bait together and to aid in mixing.
2. Mix an emetic, usually tartar emetic, with zinc phosphide and other more toxic bait formulations to protect animals other than rodents, even though acceptability of such baits to the rodents is thereby reduced.
3. Mix bait as directed. Too much poison may give the bait a strong taste or odor. Too little will not kill but may result in bait shyness. Excessive amounts of poison increase the danger to man and to domestic animals.
4. Mix baits well. Poor mixing results in non-uniform baits and poor kills and speeds development of *bait shyness.* Mechanical bait-mixing equipment is necessary where large quantities of bait are mixed routinely.
5. Clearly label poisons and mixing equipment. Do not use bait-mixing equipment for other purposes. Lock up poisons and mixing equipment when not in use. Treat all poisons with respect. Read and follow all label instructions. Avoid inhaling powders or getting poisons on hands, clothes, or utensils from which they may reach the mouth. Wear rubber gloves when handling poisons. Always mix poisons in a well-ventilated place, particularly when mixing dry ingredients.
6. If anticoagulant baits are used, they should be placed in paper, metal, or plastic pie plates or in permanent bait stations. Be liberal in baiting. For anticoagulants to be fully effective, repeated doses must be consumed by every rodent at a given location for a period of five or more consecutive days.
7. Protect animals other than domestic rodents, and shield baits from the weather under shelter or with bait boxes, boards, pipes, or cans.
8. Note locations of all bait containers so that inspections can be made rapidly and the bait that has been consumed can be quickly replaced. (Bait consumption is generally heavy right after initial placement, making daily inspection and replacement advisable for the first 3 days after regular feeding begins.)
9. At each inspection, smooth the surface of the baits so that new signs of feeding will show readily. Replace moldy, wet, caked, or insect-infested baits with fresh ones. If a bait remains undisturbed for several successive inspections, move it to an area showing fresh rodent signs.
10. Use shallow bait containers fastened to the floor or containers of sufficient weight to prevent the rodents from overturning them or dragging them to their burrows. A roofing tack driven through metal or fiber containers into the floor reduces spillage.
11. When single-dose poisons are used, wrap one-shot poison food baits in 4" x 4" paper squares to form torpedoes about the size of a large olive. These may be tossed readily into otherwise inaccessible places. If several types of bait such as meat, fish, or cereal are to be distributed at the same time, a different color of paper should be used for each of the various types of bait.
12. Be generous with baits. Too few baits, or poorly placed baits, may miss many rodents. Bait liberally where signs of rat activity are numerous and recent. In light or moderate infestations, torpedoes containing a single-dose poison, such as red squill, have given good control when applied at a minimum rate of 20 baits per private residence. As many as 100 to 200 baits may be required for premises with heavy rodent infestations.
13. Place baits in hidden sites out of reach of children and pets.
14. Inspect and rebait as needed, using another poison and another bait material when the rats become shy of the original baits.

5 (#1)

13. According to the above instructions, if you find, upon inspection, that your baits are over-run with insects, you SHOULD

    A. replace the baits with fresh baits
    B. move the baits to another station
    C. add more rodenticide to the baits and re-mix them
    D. apply the appropriate insecticide to the baits

13.____

14. According to the above instructions, if an exterminator wants to make sure he does NOT get poor kills, he SHOULD

    A. mix large quantities of baits routinely
    B. stick to one poison
    C. mix the baits well
    D. use deep bait containers that cannot be easily overturned

14.____

15. According to the above instructions, the equipment which is used for mixing bait should be

    A. cleaned routinely
    B. mechanically easy to handle
    C. easily disposable
    D. labeled clearly

15.____

16. According to the above instructions, making the surface of the bait smooth every time that you inspect the bait containers is

    A. *proper* because it disturbs the insect infestation of the bait
    B. *improper* because it will make the bait even less uniform if it was already mixed poorly
    C. *proper* because it will help you determine if new signs of feeding are present
    D. *improper* because it increases the presence of human odor on the bait and discourages rodents

16.____

17. According to the above instructions, if you are making a bait with zinc phosphide, it is MOST important to

    A. prepare a generous amount so you can bait liberally where signs of rat activity are numerous
    B. use molasses to insure that the bait will be uniform
    C. shield the bait from the weather
    D. mix an emetic with the bait

17.____

18. According to the above instructions, you should substitute one poison for another poison when the

    A. bait consumption is heavy after initial placement
    B. rodents become shy of the original baits
    C. poison is dangerous to domestic animals
    D. rodents are able to drag the baits to their burrows

18.____

19. According to the above instructions, when you handle poisons, you SHOULD

    A. use mechanical bait-making equipment
    B. wear rubber gloves
    C. never place them in paper plates
    D. always mix them with moist ingredients

20. According to the above instructions, if you plan to distribute several types of bait at the same time in the form of *torpedoes*, you SHOULD

    A. select only anticoagulant baits for this purpose
    B. reduce the possibility of bait spillage by driving a roofing tack through the container into the floor
    C. use a different color of paper for each of the various types of bait
    D. make sure that the rodent does not consume repeated doses for more than a period of five consecutive days at the same location

21. According to the above instructions, mixing too much poison in the bait

    A. may bring about bait shyness
    B. permits the exterminator to make less frequent reinspections
    C. increases the danger to other life
    D. may be necessary when anticoagulants are used

22. According to the above instructions, if grain is to be used as bait,

    A. rodents will not accept it if it is mixed with fish oil
    B. the exterminator will only be able to make *torpedoes*
    C. it will not be necessary to check the bait for fresh rodent signs
    D. a binder should also be used to aid in mixing

Questions 23-25.

DIRECTIONS: Questions 23 through 25 are to be answered SOLELY on the basis of the following paragraphs.

The German roach is the most common roach in houses in the United States. Adults are pale brown and about 1/2-inch long; both sexes have wings as long as the body, and can be distinguished from other roaches by the two dark stripes on the pronotum. The female carries its egg capsule protruding from her abdomen until the eggs are ready to hatch. This is the only common house-infesting species which carries the egg capsule for such an extended period of time. A female will usually produce 4 to 8 capsules in her lifetime. Each capsule contains 30 to 48 eggs, which hatch out in about 28 days at ordinary room temperature. The completion of the nymphal stage under room conditions requires 40 to 125 days. German roaches may live as adults for as long as 303 days.

It is stated above that the German cockroach is the most commonly encountered of the house-infesting species in the United States. The reasons for this are somewhat complex, but the understanding of some of the factors involved are basic to the practice of pest control. In the first place, the German cockroach has a larger number of eggs per capsule and a shorter hatching time than do the other species. It also requires a shorter period from hatching until sexual maturity, so that within a given period of time, a population of German roaches will produce a larger number of eggs. On the basis of this fact, we can state that this species has a high reproductive potential. Since the female carries the egg capsule during nearly the entire time that the embryos are developing within the egg, many hazards of the environment which may affect the eggs are avoided. This means that more nymphs are likely to hatch and that a larger portion of the reproductive potential is realized. The nymphs which hatch from each egg capsule tend to stay close to each other; and since they are often close to the female at time of hatching, there is a tendency for the population density to be high locally. Being smaller than most of the other roaches, they are able to conceal themselves in many places which are inaccessible to individuals of the larger species. All of these factors combined help to give the German cockroach an advantage with regard to group survival.

23. According to the above passage, the MOST important feature of the German roach which gives it an advantage over other roaches is its

    A. distinctive markings   B. immunity to disease
    C. long life span   D. power to reproduce

23._____

24. An IMPORTANT difference between an adult female German roach and an adult female of other species is the

    A. black bars or stripes which appear on the abdomen of the German roach
    B. German roach's preference for warm, moist places in which to breed
    C. long period of time during which the German roach carries the egg capsule
    D. presence of longer wings on the female German roach

24._____

25. A storeroom in a certain housing project has an infestation of German roaches, which includes 125 adult females. If the infestation is not treated and ordinary room temperature is maintained in the storeroom, how many eggs will hatch out during the lifetime of these females if they each lay 8 capsules containing 48 eggs each?

    A. 1,500   B. 48,000   C. 96,000   D. 303,000

25._____

KEY (CORRECT ANSWERS)

1.	A	11.	A
2.	B	12.	B
3.	C	13.	A
4.	C	14.	C
5.	C	15.	D
6.	B	16.	C
7.	D	17.	D
8.	A	18.	B
9.	B	19.	B
10.	B	20.	C

21. C
22. D
23. D
24. C
25. B

TEST 2

DIRECTIONS: Each question or incomplete statement is followed by several suggested answers or completions. Select the one that BEST answers the question or completes the statement. *PRINT THE LETTER OF THE CORRECT ANSWER IN THE SPACE AT THE RIGHT.*

Questions 1-10.

DIRECTIONS: Questions 1 through 10 are to be answered SOLELY on the basis of the information contained in the following passage and refer to entries that would be made on the Field Visit Report form that follows the passage.

On March 6, 2007, a crew composed of five Community Service Aides and three Pest Control Aides, under the supervision of a Crew Chief (Pest Control), made a field visit to inspect several residential buildings and a vacant lot. The purpose of the visit was to check for exposed refuse and signs of rats, mice, and insects. If conditions needed correction, they were to recommend the actions that should be taken.

The crew was driven in a department car to the first inspection site, an apartment house at 124 Grand Street, arriving at 11:30 A.M. When the crew members inspected the apartment house, they discovered rats and holes in the baseboards in several of the apartments. The landlord had not placed enough bait boxes in the basement. The Crew Chief recommended that an exterminator be scheduled to treat the building. The crew left the building at 12:05 P.M. and walked to the next inspection site at 129 Grand Street.

The crew arrived at the second site at 12:10 P.M. and left at 12:40 P.M. Because the crew found rats and roaches in the building, the Crew Chief immediately called the office and made arrangements for an exterminator to treat the building that afternoon. The Crew Chief recommended that the building should be re-inspected the following week to see if the exterminating had been successful.

The crew workers walked to the next inspection site, a vacant lot on Lucke Street, across the street from an apartment building at 350 Lucke Street. They observed that refuse covered much of the area of the vacant lot. The Crew Chief recommended that a clean-up team be scheduled to remove refuse from the lot.

The crew's last inspection of the day was a building at 300 Lucke Street. They walked to this site, arrived at 1:00 P.M., and stayed for an hour. They inspected several apartments in the building to see if a recent extermination had been successful. Upon seeing that no further work was needed at the site, they returned to their office by subway.

The Crew Chief arrived at the office at 3:00 P.M. and made out the following Field Visit Report form.

2 (#2)

FIELD VISIT REPORT FORM

1. Date_____
2. Time Arrived At First Site_____
3. Purpose of Field Visit_____
   _____
   _____

4. Number of Persons in Crew (Not including Crew Chief (Pest Control)_____
   _____

5. Transportation_____
6. Number of Sites Visited_____
7. Addresses of Sites Visited_____
   _____
   _____
   _____

8. Conditions Noted_____
   _____
   _____
   _____

9. Recommendations_____
   _____
   _____
   _____

10. Arrangements Made by Crew Chief While in the Field_____
    _____
    _____
    _____

11. Time Left Last Site_____

1. Which of the following should be entered on line 2?

   A. 11:30 A.M.   B. 12:05 P.M.
   C. 12:10 P.M.   D. 12:40 P.M.

2. Which of the following should be entered on line 3?

   A. Exterminate apartment buildings that have rats and mice
   B. Examine various sites for exposed refuse and signs of rats, mice, and Insects
   C. Inspect work done by clean-up team
   D. Clean up lots that are covered with refuse

3. The number that should be entered on line 4 is

   A. 3   B. 5   C. 8   D. 9

4. Which of the following should be entered on line 6?

   A. 3   B. 4   C. 5   D. 6

5. Each of the following should be entered on line 7 EXCEPT

   A. 124 Grand Street   B. 129 Grand Street
   C. 300 Lucke Street   D. 350 Lucke Street

6. Each of the following should be entered on line 8 EXCEPT the presence of

    A. holes in the baseboards at 124 Grand Street
    B. insects, rats, and mice at 300 Lucke Street
    C. refuse at the vacant lot on Lucke Street
    D. rats and roaches at 129 Grand Street

7. Which of the following should be entered on line 5? _____ between sites.

    A. Department car to first site, subway
    B. Subway to first site, walked
    C. Walked to first site, department car
    D. Department car to first site, walked

8. All of the following should be entered on line 9 EXCEPT

    A. extermination at 124 Grand Street to remove rats
    B. clean-up at the lot on Lucke Street to remove refuse
    C. follow-up visit at 129 Grand Street to determine success of extermination
    D. clean-up building at 300 Lucke Street to end infestation

9. Which of the following should be entered on line 10?

    A. Extermination of building at 129 Grand Street
    B. Extermination of building at 124 Grand Street
    C. Clean-up of lot on Lucke Street
    D. Clean-up of building at 300 Lucke Street

10. Which of the following should be entered on line 11?

    A. 12:40 P.M.   B. 1:00 P.M.
    C. 2:00 P.M.   D. 3:00 P.M.

Questions 11-14.

DIRECTIONS: Questions 11 through 14 are to be answered SOLELY on the basis of the following passage.

Sometimes an exterminator has to use a crowbar, for example, to open wooden crates that contain supplies which are shipped to the exterminating shop. He should know how to handle a crowbar so that he can use it safely. The danger involved in using a crowbar is that it may slip. A dull, broken crowbar is more likely to slip than one which has a sharp edge and a good *bite*. If the crowbar should slip or the object being opened should move suddenly, an exterminator's hand might be pinched or he might fall. The way in which he holds the crowbar and how he stands when using it can prevent such accidents. His hands should be dry when he uses a crowbar and, if he is wearing gloves, they should be free from grease. He should not work with the crowbar between his legs. When they are not being used, crowbars should be kept in a rack in the exterminating shop where they can not fall on someone or cause anyone to trip.

11. Of the following, the BEST title for the above passage is

    A. PROPER POSITION WHEN USING A CROWBAR
    B. TOOLS USED BY EXTERMINATORS
    C. USING A CROWBAR SAFELY
    D. WHEN TO USE A CROWBAR

12. A crowbar is MOST likely to slip if it

    A. has a good *bite*
    B. has a sharp edge
    C. is dull and broken
    D. is handled without gloves

13. Crowbars should be stored in a rack when they are not being used so that they will

    A. be easy to get at
    B. not cause accidents
    C. not be broken
    D. not be stolen

14. A worker should NOT use a crowbar if

    A. he is wearing gloves
    B. his hands are wet
    C. it has not been kept in a rack
    D. it has a sharp edge

Questions 15-17.

DIRECTIONS: Questions 15 through 17 are to be answered SOLELY on the basis of the following passage.

An exterminator should call the Fire Department for any fire except a small one in a wastebasket. This kind of fire can be put out with a fire extinguisher. If the exterminator is not sure about the size of the fire, he should not wait to find out how big it is. He should call the Fire Department at once.

Every exterminator should know what to do when a fire starts. He should know how to use the fire fighting tools in the building and how to call the Fire Department. He should also know where the nearest fire alarm box is. But the most important thing for an exterminator to do in case of fire is to avoid panic.

15. If there is a small fire in a wastebasket, an exterminator should

    A. call the Fire Department
    B. let it burn itself out
    C. open a window
    D. put it out with a fire extinguisher

16. In case of fire, the MOST important thing for an exterminator to do is to

    A. find out how big it is
    B. keep calm
    C. leave the building right away
    D. report to his boss

17. If a large fire starts while he is at work, an exterminator should always FIRST

    A. call the Fire Department
    B. notify the Housing Superintendent
    C. remove inflammables from the building
    D. use a fire extinguisher

Questions 18-19.

DIRECTIONS: Questions 18 and 19 are to be answered SOLELY on the basis of the following paragraph.

The cabinet shall be fabricated entirely of 22-gage stainless steel with #4 satin finish on all exposed surfaces. The face trim shall be one piece construction with no mitres or welding, 1" wide and 1/4" to the wall. All doors shall be mounted on heavy duty stainless steel piano hinges and have a concealed lock.

18. As used in the above paragraph, the word *fabricated* means MOST NEARLY   18.____

    A. made   B. designed   C. cut   D. plated

19. According to the above paragraph, a satin finish is to be used on surfaces   19.____

    A. to be welded
    B. that are visible
    C. on which the hinges are mounted
    D. that are to be covered

Questions 20-25.

DIRECTIONS: Questions 20 through 25 are to be answered SOLELY on the basis of the information contained in the following paragraph. Each question consists of a statement. You are to indicate whether the statement is TRUE (T) or FALSE (F).

CONTROL OF RABIES

The history of rabies in many countries proves the need for strong preventive measures. England is a good example. Rabies ran rampant in the British Isles during the American Revolution. In the 19th century, the country began to enforce strict measures: licensing all dogs, muzzling all dogs, and quarantining all incoming animals for 6 months' observation. An additional measure was the capturing and killing of all unlicensed *strays*.

As a result, rabies was completely eradicated, and similar measures have achieved the same results in Ireland, Denmark, Norway, Sweden, Australia, and Hawaii.

20. Rabies was prevalent in England about the year 1776.   20.____

21. By enforcement of strict measures in the 1800's, rabies was eliminated in England.   21.____

22. The only measures enforced in England for the control of rabies were the licensing and muzzling of all dogs.   22.____

23. Unlicensed dogs without owners were put to death when found.   23.____

24. A total of six countries, including England, obtained good results in combating rabies.   24.____

25. In three Scandinavian countries, rabies has been eliminated.   25.____

KEY (CORRECT ANSWERS)

1. A
2. B
3. C
4. B
5. D

6. B
7. D
8. D
9. A
10. C

11. C
12. C
13. B
14. B
15. D

16. B
17. A
18. A
19. B
20. T

21. T
22. F
23. T
24. F
25. T

INTERPRETING STATISTICAL DATA GRAPHS, CHARTS AND TABLES

EXAMINATION SECTION
TEST 1

DIRECTIONS: Each question or incomplete statement is followed by several suggested answers or completions. Select the one that BEST answers the question or completes the statement. *PRINT THE LETTER OF THE CORRECT ANSWER IN THE SPACE AT THE RIGHT.*

Questions 1-3.

DIRECTIONS: Questions 1 through 3 are to be answered SOLELY on the basis of the information given below.

Assume that at various hours of a typical day the amounts of chlorine residual in parts per million (ppm) at a certain water treatment plant are as shown in the following graph.

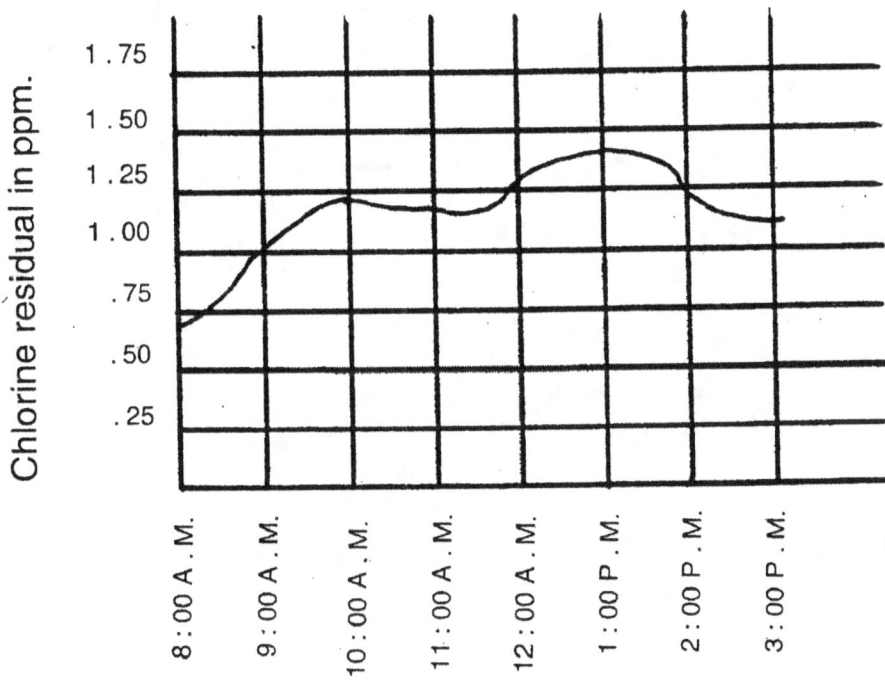

1. According to the graph, the chlorine residual measured in ppm at 9:00 A.M. was MOST NEARLY 1._____

   A. .70   B. .75   C. 1.00   D. 1.25

2. The MAXIMUM chlorine residual between 8:00 A.M. and 3:00 P.M. was MOST NEARLY _____ ppm. 2._____

   A. .68   B. 1.10   C. 1.25   D. 1.37

2 (#1)

3. According to the graph, between the hours of 12:00 Noon and 1:00 P.M., the chlorine residual was

    A. always increasing
    B. always decreasing
    C. increasing, then decreasing
    D. decreasing, then increasing

3.____

KEY (CORRECT ANSWERS)

1. C
2. D
3. A

TEST 2

Questions 1-3.

DIRECTIONS: Questions 1 through 3 are to be answered SOLELY on the basis of the information given below.

Assume that a certain water treatment plant has consumed quantities of chemicals E and F over a five-week period, as indicated in the following table.

Time Period	Number of 100-pound sacks consumed	
	Chemical E	Chemical F
Week 1	5	4
Week 2	7	5
Week 3	6	5
Week 4	8	6
Week 5	6	4

1. The TOTAL number of pounds of Chemical E consumed at the end of the first three weeks is

    A. 180   B. 320   C. 1,400   D. 1,800

2. According to the table, the week in which the MOST chemicals were consumed was week

    A. 2   B. 3   C. 4   D. 5

3. According to the table, the AVERAGE number of sacks of Chemical F consumed over the first four weeks was

    A. 4   B. 5   C. 6   D. 7

KEY (CORRECT ANSWERS)

1. D
2. C
3. B

TEST 3

Questions 1-5.

DIRECTIONS: Questions 1 through 5 are to be answered on the basis of the information given in the table below.

Date of Water Meter Reading	Water Meter Readings in Cubic Feet				
	Meter 1	Meter 2	Meter 3	Meter 4	Meter 5
Dec. 31, 2016	12,416	88,990	64,312	26,985	30,057
June 30, 2017	23,094	98,806	71,527	27,336	30,057
Dec. 31, 2017	33,011	07,723	79,292	27,848	30,618
June 30, 2018	42,907	16,915	87,208	28,286	31,247
Dec. 31, 2018	52,603	26,456	95,244	28,742	31,740

NOTE: The maximum readings of each of the above five meters is 99,999 cubic feet. Above that reading, the meters start registering from zero.

NOTE: Assume that the maximum water consumption between consecutive readings is less than 100,000 cubic feet.

1. The meter which showed the LOWEST water consumption for the period June 30, 2018 to December 31, 2018 is Meter

   A. 2   B. 3   C. 4   D. 5

2. The amount of water consumed between June 30, 2017 and December 31, 2017 by the consumers metered by Meter 2 is _____ cubic feet.

   A. 7,723   B. 8,917   C. 91,083   D. 107,723

3. The meter which showed the GREATEST water consumption over the time period December 31, 2016 to December 31, 2018 is Meter

   A. 1   B. 2   C. 3   D. 4

4. The meter which showed EXACTLY the same water consumption for 2018 as in 2017 is Meter

   A. 1   B. 2   C. 4   D. 5

5. The meter which shows EXACTLY TWICE as much water consumption in 2018 as compared to the consumption in 2017 is Meter

   A. 1   B. 3   C. 4   D. 5

KEY (CORRECT ANSWERS)

1. C
2. B
3. A
4. B
5. D

TEST 4

Questions 1-3.

DIRECTIONS: Questions 1 through 3 are to be answered ONLY on the basis of the information given below.

At midnight of each day, readings are made of gas consumption meters. Readings for 8 days are as follows:

Sunday	6873 cu.ft.	Thursday	3256 cu.ft.
Monday	8147 cu.ft.	Friday	4962 cu.ft.
Tuesday	0065 cu.ft.	Saturday	6823 cu.ft.
Wednesday	1480 cu.ft.	Sunday	7179 cu.ft.

1. According to the above table, the total gas consumed for the week was MOST NEARLY _____ cubic feet.

   A. 1,000   B. 4,000   C. 7,000   D. 10,000

2. Gas consumption for Tuesday was MOST NEARLY _____ cubic feet.

   A. 500   B. 1,000   C. 2,000   D. 8,000

3. The day on which gas consumption was LOWEST was

   A. Monday   B. Tuesday   C. Wednesday   D. Thursday

KEY (CORRECT ANSWERS)

1. D
2. C
3. A

PREPARING WRITTEN MATERIAL
EXAMINATION SECTION
TEST 1

DIRECTIONS: Each question consists of a sentence which may or may not be an example of good English usage. Examine each sentence, considering grammar, punctuation, spelling, capitalization, and awkwardness. Then choose the correct statement about it from the four choices below it. If the English usage in the sentence given is better than any of the changes suggested in choices B, C, or D, pick choice A. (Do not pick a choice that will change the meaning of the sentence.) *PRINT THE LETTER OF THE CORRECT ANSWER IN THE SPACE AT THE RIGHT.*

1. We attended a staff conference on Wednesday the new safety and fire rules were discussed.   1.____
   A. This is an example of acceptable writing.
   B. The words "safety," "fire," and "rules" should begin with capital letters.
   C. There should be a comma after the word "Wednesday."
   D. There should be a period after the word "Wednesday" and the word "the" should begin with a capital letter.

2. Neither the dictionary or the telephone directory could be found in the office library.   2.____
   A. This is an example of acceptable writing.
   B. The word "or" should be changed to "nor."
   C. The word "library" should be spelled "libery."
   D. The word "neither" should be changed to "either."

3. The report would have been typed correctly if the typist could read the draft.   3.____
   A. This is an example of acceptable writing.
   B. The word "would" should be removed.
   C. The word "have" should be inserted after the word "could."
   D. The word "correctly" should be changed to "correct."

4. The supervisor brought the reports and forms to an employees desk.   4.____
   A. This is an example of acceptable writing.
   B. The word "brought" should be changed to "took."
   C. There should be a comma after the word "reports" and a comma after the word "forms."
   D. The word "employees" should be spelled "employee's."

5. It's important for all the office personnel to submit their vacation schedules on time.   5.____
   A. This is an example of acceptable writing.
   B. The word "It's" should be spelled "Its."
   C. The word "their" should be spelled "they're."
   D. The word "personnel" should be spelled "personal."

6. The report, along with the accompanying documents, were submitted for review.
   A. This is an example of acceptable writing.
   B. The words "were submitted" should be changed to "was submitted."
   C. The word "accompanying" should be spelled "accompaning."
   D. The comma after the word "report" should be taken out.

7. If others must use your files, be certain that they understand how the system works, but insist that you do all the filing and refiling.
   A. This is an example of acceptable writing.
   B. There should be a period after the word "works," and the word "but" should start a new sentence.
   C. The words "filing" and "refiling" should be spelled "fileing" and "refileing."
   D. There should be a comma after the word "but."

8. The appeal was not considered because of its late arrival.
   A. This is an example of acceptable writing.
   B. The word "its" should be changed to "it's."
   C. The word "its" should be changed to "the."
   D. The words "late arrival" should be changed to "arrival late."

9. The letter must be read carefuly to determine under which subject it should be filed.
   A. This is an example of acceptable writing.
   B. The word "under" should be changed to "at."
   C. The word "determine" should be spelled "determin."
   D. The word "carefuly" should be spelled "carefully."

10. He showed potential as an office manager, but he lacked skill in delegating work.
    A. This is an example of acceptable writing.
    B. The word "delegating" should be spelled "delagating."
    C. The word "potential" should be spelled "potencial."
    D. The words "he lacked" should be changed to "was lacking."

KEY (CORRECT ANSWERS)

1.	D	6.	B
2.	B	7.	A
3.	C	8.	A
4.	D	9.	D
5.	A	10.	A

TEST 2

DIRECTIONS: Each question consists of a sentence which may or may not be an example of good English usage. Examine each sentence, considering grammar, punctuation, spelling, capitalization, and awkwardness. Then choose the correct statement about it from the four choices below it. If the English usage in the sentence given is better than any of the changes suggested in choices B, C, or D, pick choice A. (Do not pick a choice that will change the meaning of the sentence.) *PRINT THE LETTER OF THE CORRECT ANSWER IN THE SPACE AT THE RIGHT.*

1. The supervisor wants that all staff members report to the office at 9:00 A.M. 1.____
    A. This is an example of acceptable writing.
    B. The word "that" should be removed and the word "to" should be inserted after the word "members."
    C. There should be a comma after the word "wants" and a comma after the word "office."
    D. The word "wants" should be changed to "want" and the word "shall" should be inserted after the word "members."

2. Every morning the clerk opens the office mail and distributes it. 2.____
    A. This is an example of acceptable writing.
    B. The word "opens" should be changed to "open."
    C. The word "mail" should be changed to "letters."
    D. The word "it" should be changed to "them."

3. The secretary typed more fast on a desktop computer than on a laptop computer. 3.____
    A. This is an example of acceptable writing.
    B. The words "more fast" should be changed to "faster."
    C. There should be a comma after the words "desktop computer."
    D. The word "than" should be changed to "then."

4. The new stenographer needed a desk a computer, a chair and a blotter. 4.____
    A. This is an example of acceptable writing.
    B. The word "blotter" should be spelled "blodder."
    C. The word "stenographer" should begin with a capital letter.
    D. There should be a comma after the word "desk."

5. The recruiting officer said, "There are many different goverment jobs available." 5.____
    A. This is an example of acceptable writing.
    B. The word "There" should not be capitalized.
    C. The word "government" should be spelled "government."
    D. The comma after the word "said" should be removed.

6. He can recommend a mechanic whose work is reliable. 6.____
    A. This is an example of acceptable writing.
    B. The word "reliable" should be spelled "relyable."
    C. The word "whose" should be spelled "who's."
    D. The word "mechanic should be spelled "mecanic."

105

7. She typed quickly; like someone who had not a moment to lose.
   A. This is an example of acceptable writing.
   B. The word "not" should be removed.
   C. The semicolon should be changed to a comma.
   D. The word "quickly" should be placed before instead of after the word "typed."

8. She insisted that she had to much work to do.
   A. This is an example of acceptable writing.
   B. The word "insisted" should be spelled "incisted."
   C. The word "to" used in front of "much" should be spelled "too."
   D. The word "do" should be changed to "be done."

9. He excepted praise from his supervisor for a job well done.
   A. This is an example of acceptable writing.
   B. The word "excepted" should be spelled "accepted."
   C. The order of the words "well done" should be changed to "done well."
   D. There should be a comma after the word "supervisor."

10. What appears to be intentional errors in grammar occur several times in the passage.
    A. This is an example of acceptable writing.
    B. The word "occur" should be spelled "occurr."
    C. The word "appears" should be changed to "appear."
    D. The phrase "several times" should be changed to "from time to time."

KEY (CORRECT ANSWERS)

1.	B	6.	A
2.	A	7.	C
3.	B	8.	C
4.	D	9.	B
5.	C	10.	C

TEST 3

DIRECTIONS: Each question consists of a sentence which may or may not be an example of good English usage. Examine each sentence, considering grammar, punctuation, spelling, capitalization, and awkwardness. Then choose the correct statement about it from the four choices below it. If the English usage in the sentence given is better than any of the changes suggested in choices B, C, or D, pick choice A. (Do not pick a choice that will change the meaning of the sentence.) *PRINT THE LETTER OF THE CORRECT ANSWER IN THE SPACE AT THE RIGHT.*

1. The clerk could have completed the assignment on time if he knows where these materials were located.
    A. This is an example of acceptable writing.
    B. The word "knows" should be replaced by "had known."
    C. The word "were" should be replaced by "had been."
    D. The words "where these materials were located" should be replaced by "the location of these materials."

2. All employees should be given safety training. Not just those who accidents.
    A. This is an example of acceptable writing.
    B. The period after the word "training" should be changed to a colon.
    C. The period after the word "training" should be changed to a semicolon, and the first letter of the word "Not" should be changed to a small "n."
    D. The period after the word "training" should be changed to a comma, and the first letter of the word "Not" should be changed to a small "n."

3. This proposal is designed to promote employee awareness of the suggestion program, to encourage employee participation in the program, and to increase the number of suggestions submitted.
    A. This is an example of acceptable writing.
    B. The word "proposal" should be spelled "proposal."
    C. The words "to increase the number of suggestions submitted" should be changed to "an increase in the number of suggestions is expected."
    D. The word "promote" should be changed to "enhance" and the word "increase" should be changed to "add to."

4. The introduction of inovative managerial techniques should be preceded by careful analysis of the specific circumstances and conditions in each department.
    A. This is an example of acceptable writing.
    B. The word "technique" should be spelled "techneques."
    C. The word "inovative" should be spelled "innovative."
    D. A comma should be placed after the word "circumstances" and after the word "conditions."

5. This occurrence indicates that such criticism embarrasses him. 5.____
   A. This is an example of acceptable writing.
   B. The word "occurrence" should be spelled "occurence."
   C. The word "criticism" should be spelled "critisism.
   D. The word "embarrasses" should be spelled "embarasses.

KEY (CORRECT ANSWERS)

1. B
2. D
3. A
4. C
5. A

PREPARING WRITTEN MATERIAL

PARAGRAPH REARRANGEMENT
COMMENTARY

The sentences that follow are in scrambled order. You are to rearrange them in proper order and indicate the letter choice containing the correct answer at the space at the right.

Each group of sentences in this section is actually a paragraph presented in scrambled order. Each sentence in the group has a place in that paragraph; no sentence is to be left out. You are to read each group of sentences and decide upon the best order in which to put the sentences so as to form a well-organized paragraph.

The questions in this section measure the ability to solve a problem when all the facts relevant to its solution are not given.

More specifically, certain positions of responsibility and authority require the employee to discover connection between events sometimes, apparently, unrelated. In order to do this, the employee will find it necessary to correctly infer that unspecified events have probably occurred or are likely to occur. This ability becomes especially important when action must be taken on incomplete information.

Accordingly, these questions require competitors to choose among several suggested alternatives, each of which presents a different sequential arrangement of the events. Competitors must choose the MOST logical of the suggested sequences.

In order to do so, they may be required to draw on general knowledge to infer missing concepts or events that are essential to sequencing the given events. Competitors should be careful to infer only what is essential to the sequence. The plausibility of the wrong alternatives will always require the inclusion of unlikely events or of additional chains of events which are NOT essential to sequencing the given events.

It's very important to remember that you are looking for the best of the four possible choices, and that the best choice of all may not even be one of the answers you're given to choose from.

There is no one right way to solve these problems. Many people have found it helpful to first write out the order of the sentences, as they would have arranged them, on their scrap paper before looking at the possible answers. If their optimum answer is there, this can save them some time. If it isn't, this method can still give insight into solving the problem. Others find it most helpful to just go through each of the possible choices, contrasting each as they go along. You should use whatever method feels comfortable and works for you.

While most of these types of questions are not that difficult, we've added a higher percentage of the difficult type, just to give you more practice. Usually there are only one or two questions on this section that contain such subtle distinctions that you're unable to answer confidently. And you then may find yourself stuck deciding between two possible choices, neither of which you're sure about.

PREPARING WRITTEN MATERIAL
PARAGRAPH REARRANGEMENT
EXAMINATION SECTION
TEST 1

DIRECTIONS: The following groups of sentences need to be arranged in an order that makes sense. Select the letter preceding the sequence that represents the best sentence order. *PRINT THE LETTER OF THE CORRECT ANSWER IN THE SPACE AT THE RIGHT.*

1.
   I. The ostrich egg shell's legendary toughness makes it an excellent substitute for certain types of dishes or dinnerware, and in parts of Africa ostrich shells are cut and decorated for use as containers for water.
   II. Since prehistoric times, people have used the enormous egg of the ostrich as a part of their diet, a practice which has required much patience and hard work—to hard boil an ostrich egg takes about four hours.
   III. Opening the egg's shell, which is rock hard and nearly an inch thick, requires heavy tools, such as a saw or chisel; from inside, a baby ostrich must use a hornlike projection on its beak as a miniature pick-axe to escape from the egg.
   IV. The offspring of all higher-order animals originate from single egg cells that are carried by mothers, and most of these eggs are relatively small, often microscopic.
   V. The egg of the African ostrich, however, weighs a massive thirty pounds, making it the largest single cell on earth, and a common object of human curiosity and wonder.
   The BEST order is:
   A. V, IV, I, II, III   B. I, IV, V, III, II   C. IV, II, III, V, I   D. IV, V, II, III, I

   1.____

2.
   I. Typically only a few feet high on the open sea, individual tsunami have been known to circle the entire globe two or three times if their progress is not interrupted, but are not usually dangerous until they approach the shallow water that surrounds land masses.
   II. Some of the most terrifying and damaging hazards caused by earthquakes are tsunami, which were once called "tidal waves"—a poorly chosen name, since these waves have nothing to do with tides.
   III. Then a wave, slowed by the sudden drag on the lower part of its moving water column, will pile upon itself, sometimes reaching a height of over 100 feet.
   IV. Tsunami (Japanese for "great harbor wave") are seismic waves that are caused by earthquakes near oceanic trenches, and once triggered, can travel up to 600 miles an hour on the open ocean.
   V. A land-shoaling tsunami is capable of extraordinary destruction; some tsunami have deposited large boats miles inland, washed out two-foot-thick seawalls, and scattered locomotive trains over long distances.
   The BEST order is:
   A. IV, I, III, II, V   B. I, III, IV, II, V   C. V, I, III, II, IV   D. II, IV, I, III, V

   2.____

3.
I. Soon, by the 1940s, jazz was the most popular type of music among American intellectuals and college students.
II. In the early days of jazz, it was considered "lowdown" music, or music that was played only in rough, disreputable bars and taverns.
III. However, jazz didn't take too long to develop from early ragtime melodies into more complex, sophisticated forms, such as Charlie Parker's "bebop" style of jazz.
IV. After charismatic band leaders such as Duke Ellington and Count Basie brought jazz to a larger audience, and jazz continued to evolve into more complicated forms, white audiences began to accept and even to enjoy the new American art form.
V. Many white Americans, who then dictated the tastes of society, were wary of music that was played almost exclusively in black clubs in the poorer sections of cities and towns.
The BEST order is:
A. V, IV, III, II, I   B. II, V, III, IV, I   C. IV, V, III, I, II   D. I, II, IV, III, V

3._____

4.
I. Then, hanging in a windless place, the magnetized end of the needle would always point to the south.
II. The needle could then be balanced on the rim of a cup, or the edge of a fingernail, but this balancing act was hard to maintain, and the needle often fell off.
III. Other needles would point to the north, and it was important for any traveler finding his way with a compass to remember which kind of magnetized needle he was carrying.
IV. To make some of the earliest compasses in recorded history, ancient Chinese "magicians" would rub a needle with a piece of magnetized iron called a lodestone.
V. A more effective method of keeping the needle free to swing with its magnetic pull was to attach a strand of silk to the center of the needle with a tiny piece of wax.
The BEST order is:
A. IV, II, V, I, III   B. IV, III, V, II, I   C. IV, V, II, I, III   D. IV, I, III, V, II

4._____

5.
I The now-famous first mate of the *H.M.S. Bounty*, Fletcher Christian, founded one of the world's most peculiar civilizations in 1790.
II. The men knew they had just committed a crime for which they could be hanged, so they set sail for Pitcairn, a remote, abandoned island in the far eastern region of the Polynesian archipelago, accompanied by twelve Polynesian women and six men.
III. In a mutiny that has become legendary, Christian and the others forced Captain Bligh into a lifeboat and set him adrift off the coast of Tonga in April of 1789.
IV. In early 1790, the *Bounty* landed at Pitcairn Island, where the men lived out the rest of their lives and founded an isolated community which to this day includes direct descendants of Christian and the other Crewmen.

5._____

V. The *Bounty*, commanded by Captain William Bligh, was in the middle of a global voyage, and Christian and his shipmates had come to the conclusion that Bligh was a reckless madman who would lead them to their deaths unless they took the ship from him.

The BEST order is:
  A. IV, V, III, II, I   B. I, III, V, II, IV   C. I, V, III, II, IV   D. III, I, V, IV, II

6. I. But once the vines had been led to make orchids, the flowers had to be carefully hand-pollinated, because unpollinated orchids usually lasted less than a day, wilting and dropping off the vine before it had even become dark.
    II. The Totonac farmers discovered that looping a vine back around once it reached a five-foot height on its host tree would cause the vine to flower.
    III. Though they knew how to process the fruit pods and extract vanilla's flavoring agent, the Totonacs also knew that a wild vanilla vine did not produce abundant flowers or fruit.
    IV. Wild vines climbed along the trunks and canopies of trees, and this constant upward growth diverted most of the vine's energy to making leaves instead of the orchid flowers that once pollinated, would produce the flavorful pods.
    V. Hundreds of years before vanilla became a prized food flavoring in Europe and the Western World, the Totonac Indians of the Mexican Gulf Coast were skilled cultivators of the vanilla vine, whose fruit they literally worshipped as a goddess.

    The BEST order is:
      A. II, III, IV, I, V   B. II, IV, III, I, V   C. V, III, IV, II, I   D. III, IV, I, II, V

7. I. Once airborne, the spider is at the mercy of the air currents—usually the spider takes a brief journey, traveling close to the ground, but some have been found in air samples collected as high as 10,000 feet, or been reported landing on ships far out at sea.
    II. Once a young spider has hatched, it must leave the environment into which it was born as quickly as possible, in order to avoid competing with its hundreds of brothers and sisters for food.
    III. The silk rises into warm air currents, and as soon as the pull feels adequate the spider lets go and drifts up into the air, suspended from the silk strand in the same way that a person might parasail.
    IV. To help young spiders do this, many species have adapted a practice known as "aerial dispersal," or, in common speech, "ballooning."
    V. A spider that wants to leave its surroundings quickly will climb to the top of a grass system or twig, face into the wind, and aim its back end into the air, releasing a long stream of silk from the glands near the tip of its abdomen.

    The BEST order is:
      A. V, IV, II, III, I   B. V, II, IV, I, III   C. II, V, IV, III, I   D. II, IV, V, III, I

8. I. For about a year, Tycho worked at a castle in Prague with a scientist named Johannes Kepler, but their association was cut short by another argument that drove Kepler out of the castle, to later develop, on his own, the theory of planetary orbits.
    II. Tycho found life without a nose embarrassing, so he made a new nose for himself out of silver, which reportedly remained glued to his face for the rest of his life.
    III. Tycho Brahe, the 17th-century Danish astronomer, is today more famous for his odd and arrogant personality than for any contribution he has made to our knowledge of the stars and planets.
    IV. Early in his career, as a student at Rostock University, Tycho got into an argument with another student about who was the better mathematician, and the two became so angry that the argument turned into a sword fight, during which Tycho's nose was sliced off.
    V. Later in his life, Tycho's arrogance may have kept him from playing a part in one of the greatest astronomical discoveries in history: the elliptical orbits of the solar system's planets.
    The BEST order is:
    A. I, IV, II, III, V   B. IV, II, III, V, I   C. IV, II, I, III, V   D. III, IV, II, V, I

9. I. The processionaries are so used to this routine that if a person picks up the end of a silk line and brings it back to the origin—creating a closed circle—the caterpillars may travel around and around for days, sometimes starving or freezing, without changing course.
    II. Rather than relying on sight or sound, the other caterpillars, who are lined up end-to-end behind the leader, travel to and from their nests by walking on this silk line, and each will reinforce it by laying down its own marking line as it passes over.
    III. In order to insure the safety of individuals, the processionary caterpillar nests in a tree with dozens of other caterpillars, and at night, when it is safest, they all leave together in search of food.
    IV. The processionary caterpillar of the European continent is a perfect illustration of how much some inspect species rely on instinct in their daily routines.
    V. As they leave their nests, the processionaries form a single-file line behind a leader who spins and lays out a silk line to mark the chosen path.
    The BEST order is:
    A. IV, III, V, II, I   B. III, V, IV, II, I   C. III, V, II, I, IV   D. IV, V, III, I, II

10. I. Often, the child is also given a handcrafted walker or push cart, to provide support for its first upright explorations.
    II. In traditional Indian families, a child's first steps are celebrated as a ceremonial event, rooted in ancient myth.
    III. These carts are often intricately designed to resemble the chariot of Krishna, an important figure in Indian mythology.
    IV. The sound of these anklet bells is intended to mimic the footsteps of the legendary child Rama, who is celebrated in devotional songs throughout India.

V. When the child's parents see that the child is ready to begin walking, they will fit it with specially designed ankle bracelets, adorned with gently ringing bells.

The BEST order is:
A. II, III, IV, I, V B. II, V, III, I, IV C. V, IV, I, III, II D. V, III, II, I, IV

11. I. The settlers planted Osage oranges all across Middle America, and today long lines and rectangles of Osage orange trees can still be seen on the prairies, running along the former boundaries of farms that no longer exist.
    II. After trying sod walls and water-filled ditches with no success, American farmers began to look for a plant that was adaptable to prairie weather, and that could be trimmed into a hedge that was "pig-tight, horse-high, and bull-strong."
    III. The tree, so named because it bore a large (but inedible) fruit the size of an orange, was among the sturdiest and hardiest of American trees, and was prized among Native Americans for the strength and flexibility of bows which were made from its wood.
    IV. The first people to practice agriculture on the American flatlands were faced with an important problem: what would they use to fence their land in a place that was almost entirely without trees or rocks?
    V. Finally, an Illinois farmer brought the settlers a tree that was native to the land between the Red and Arkansas rivers, a tree called the Osage orange.

    The BEST order is:
    A. II, I, V, III, IV B. I, II, III, IV, V C. IV, II, V, III, I D. IV, II, I, III, V

11._____

12. I. After about ten minutes of such spirited and complicated activity, the head dancer is free to make up his or her own movements while maintaining the interest of the New Year's crowd.
    II. The dancer will then perform a series of leg kicks, while at the same time operating the lion's mouth with his own hand and moving the ears and eyes by means of a string which is attached to the dancer's own mouth.
    III. The most difficult role of this dance belongs to the one who controls the lion's head; this person must lead all the other "parts" of the lion through the choreographed segments of the dance.
    IV. The head dancer begins with a complex series of steps. alternately stepping forward with the head raised, and then retreating a few steps while lowering the head, a movement that is intended to create the impression that the lion is keeping a watchful eye for anything evil.
    V. When performing a traditional Chinese New Year's lion dance, several performers must fit themselves inside a large lion costume and work together to enact different parts of the dance.

    The BEST order is:
    A. V, III, IV, II, I B. III, IV, II, V, I C. III, I, V, IV, II D. IV, II, III, V, I

12._____

13.
   I. For many years the shell of the chambered nautilus was treasured in Europe for its beauty and intricacy, but collectors were unaware that they were in possession of the structure that marked a "missing link" in the evolution of marine mollusks.
   II. The nautilus, however, evolved a series of enclosed chambers in its shell, and invented a new use for the structure: the shell began to serve as a buoyancy device.
   III. Equipped with this new flotation device, the nautilus did not need the single, muscular foot of its predecessors, but instead developed flaps, tentacles, and a gentle form of jet propulsion that transformed it into the first mollusk able to take command of its own density and explore a three-dimensional world.
   IV. By pumping and adjusting air pressure into the chambers, the nautilus could spend the day resting on the bottom, and then rise toward the surface at night in search of food.
   V. The nautilus shell looks like a large snail shell, similar to those of its ancestors, who used their shells as protective coverings while they were anchored to the sea floor.

   The BEST order is:
   A. V, II, IV, I, III   B. V, I, II, III, IV   C. I, II, V, III, IV   D. I, V, II, IV, III

14.
   I. While France and England battled for control of the region, the Acadiens prospered on the fertile farmland, which was finally secured by England in 1713.
   II. Early in the 17th century, settlers from Western France founded a colony called Acadie in what is now the Canadian province of Nova Scotia.
   III. At this time, English officials feared the presence of spies among the Acadiens who might be loyal to their French homeland, and the Acadiens were deported to spots along the Atlantic and Caribbean shores of America.
   IV. The French settlers remained on this land, under English rule, for around forty years, until the beginning of the French and Indian War, another conflict between France and England.
   V. As the Acadien refugees drifted toward a final home in Southern Louisiana, neighbors shortened their name to "Cadien," and finally "Cajun," the name which the descendants of early Acadiens still call themselves.

   The BEST order is:
   A. I, IV, II, III, V   B. II, I, III, V, IV   C. II, I, IV, III, V   D. V, II, III, IV, I

15.
   I. Traditional households in the Eastern and Western regions of Africa serve two meals a day—one at around noon, and the other in the evening.
   II. The starch is then used in the way that Americans might use a spoon, to scoop up a portion of the main dish on the person's plate.
   III. The reason for the starch's inclusion in every meal has to do with taste as well as nutrition; African food can be very spicy, and the starch is known to cool the burning effect of the main dish.
   IV. When serving these meals, the main dish is usually served on individual plates, and the starch is served on a communal plate, from which diners break off a piece of bread or scoop rice or fufu in their fingers.

V. The typical meals usually consist of a thick stew or soup as the main course, and an accompanying starch—either bread, rice, or *fufu*, a starchy grain paste similar in consistency to mashed potatoes.
The BEST order is:
A. V, II, III, IV, I   B. V, I, IV, III, II   C. I, IV, V, III, II   D. I, V, IV, II, III

16. I. In the early days of the American Midwest, Indiana settlers sometimes came together to hold an event called an apple peeling, where neighboring settlers gathered at the homestead of a host family to help prepare the hosts' apple crop for cooking, canning, and making apple butter.
II. At the beginning of the event, each peeler sat down in front of a ten- or twenty-gallon stone jar and was given a crock of apples and a paring knife.
III. Once a peeler had finished with a crock, another was placed next to him; if the peeler was an unmarried man, he kept a strict count of the number of apples he had peeled, because the winner was allowed to kiss the girl of his choice.
IV. The peeling usually ended by 9:30 in the evening, when the neighbors gathered in the host family's parlor for a dance social.
V. The apples were peeled, cored, and quartered, and then placed into the jar.
The BEST order is:
A. I, V, III, IV, II   B. II, V, III, IV, I   C. I, II, V, III, IV   D. II, I, V, IV, III

16.____

17. I. If your pet turtle is a land turtle and is native to temperate climates, it will stop eating some time in October, which should be your cue to prepare the turtle for hibernation.
II. The box should then be covered with a wire screen, which will protect the turtle from any rodents or predators that might want to take advantage of a motionless and helpless animal.
III. When your turtle hasn't eaten for a while and appears ready to hibernate, it should be moved to its winter quarters, most likely a cellar or garage, where the temperature should range between 40° and 45°F.
IV. Instead of feeding the turtle, you should bathe it every day in warm water, to encourage the turtle to empty its intestines in preparation for its long winter sleep.
V. Here the turtle should be placed in a well-ventilated box whose bottom is covered with a moisture-absorbing layer of clay beads, and then filled three-fourths full with almost dry peat moss or wood chips, into which the turtle will burrow and sleep for several months.
The BEST order is:
A. I, IV, III, V, II   B. III, IV, II, V, I   C. III, II, IV, I, V   D. IV, V, II, III, I

17.____

18. I. Once he has reached the nest, the hunter uses two sturdy bamboo poles like huge chopsticks to pull the next away from the mountainside, into a large basket that will be lowered to people waiting below.
II. The world's largest honeybees colonize the Nealese mountainsides, building honeycombs as large as a person on sheer rock faces that are often hundreds of feet high.

18.____

III. In the remote mountain country of Nepal, a small band of "honey hunters" carry out a tradition so ancient that 10,000 year-old drawings of the practice have been found in the caves of Nepal.
IV. To harvest the honey and beeswax from these combs, a honey hunter climbs above the nests, lowers a long bamboo-fiber ladder over the cliff, and then climbs down.
V. Throughout this dangerous practice, the hunter is stung repeatedly, and only the veterans, with skin that has been toughened over the years, are able to return from a hunt without the painful swelling caused by stings.

The BEST order is:
A. II, IV, III, V, I   B. II, IV, I, V, III   C. V, III, II, IV, I   D. III, II, IV, I, V

19.
I. After the Romans left Britain, there were relentless attacks on the islands from the barbarian tribes of northern Germany—the Angles, Saxons, and Jutes.
II. As the empire weakened, Roman soldiers withdrew from Britain, leaving behind a country that continued to practice the Christian religion that had been introduced by the Romans.
III. Early Latin writings tell of a Christian warrior named Arturius (Arthur, in English) who led the British citizens to defeat these barbarian invades, and brought an extended period of peace to the lands of Britain.
IV. Long ago, the British Isles were part of the far-flung Roman Empire that extended across most of Europe and into Africa and Asia.
V. The romantic legend of King Arthur and his knights of the Round Table, one of the most popular and widespread stories of all time, appears to have some foundation in history.

The BEST order is:
A. V, IV, III, II, I   B. V, IV, II, I, III   C. IV, V, II, III, I   D. IV, III, II, I, V

20.
I. The cylinder was allowed to cool until it could stand on its own, and then it was cut from the tube and split down the side with a single straight cut.
II. Nineteenth-century glassmakers, who had not yet discovered the glazier's modern techniques for making panes of glass, had to create a method for converting their blown gas into flat sheets.
III. The bubble was then pierced at the end to make a hole that opened up while the glassmaker gently spun it, creating a cylinder of glass.
IV. Turned on its side and laid on a conveyor belt, the cylinder was strengthened, or tempered, by being heated again and cooled very slowly, eventually flattening out into a single rectangular of glass.
V. To do this, the glassmaker dipped the end of a long tube into melted glass and blew into the other end of the tube, creating an expanding bubble of glass.

The BEST order is:
A. II, V, III, IV, I   B. II, IV, V, III, I   C. III, V, II, IV, I   D. III, I, IV, V, II

21. I. The splints are almost always hidden, but horses are occasionally born whose splinted toes project from the leg on either side, just above the hoof.
    II. The second and fourth toes remained, but shrank to thin splints of bone that fused invisibly to the horse's leg bone.
    III. Horses are unique among mammals, having evolved feet that each end in what is essentially a single toe, capped by a large, sturdy hoof.
    IV. Julius Caesar, an emperor of ancient Rome, was said to have owned one of these three-toed horses, and considered it so special that he would not permit anyone else to ride it.
    V. Though the horse's earlier ancestors possessed the traditional mammalian set of five toes on each foot, the horse has retained only its third toe; its first and fifth toes disappeared completely as the horse evolved.
    The BEST order is:
    A. III, V, II, I, IV   B. V, III, II, IV, I   C. III, II, V, I, IV   D. V, II, III, I, IV

21.____

22. I. The new building materials—some of which are twenty feet long, and weigh nearly six tons—were transported to Pohnpei on rafts, and were brought into their present position by using hibiscus fiber ropes and leverage to move the stone columns upward along the inclined trunks of coconut palm trees.
    II. The ancestors built great fires to heat the stone, and then poured cool seawater on the columns, which caused the stone to contract and split along natural fracture lines.
    III. The now-abandoned enclave of Nan Madol, a group of 92 man-made islands off the shore of the Micronesian island of Pohnpei, is estimated to have been built around the year 500 A.D.
    IV. The islanders say their ancestors quarried stone columns from a nearby island, where large basalt columns were formed by the cooling of molten lava.
    V. The structures of Nan Madol are remarkable for the sheer size of some of the stone "longs" or columns that were used to create the walls of the offshore community, and today anthropologists can only rely on the information of existing local people for clues about how Nan Madol was built.
    The BEST order is:
    A. V, IV, III, II, I   B. V, III, I, IV, II   C. III, V, IV, II, I   D. III, I, IV, II, V

22.____

23. I. One of the most easily manipulated substances on earth, glass can be made into ceramic tiles that are composed of over 90% air.
    II. NASA's space shuttles are the first spacecraft ever designed to leave and re-enter the earth's atmosphere while remaining intact.
    III. These ceramic tiles are such effective insulators that when a tile emerges from the oven in which it was fired, it can be held safely in a person's hand by the edges while its interior still glows at a temperature well over 2000°F.
    IV. Eventually, the engineers were led to a material that is as old as our most ancient civilization.
    V. Because the temperature during atmospheric re-entry is so incredibly hot, it took NASA's engineers some time to find a substance capable of protecting the shuttles.

22.____

The BEST order is:
 A. V, II, I, II, IV   B. II, V, IV, I, III   C. II, III, I, IV, V   D. V, IV, III, I, II

24. I. The secret to teaching any parakeet to talk is patience, and the understanding that when a bird talks," it is simply imitating what it hears, rather than putting ideas into words.
    II. You should stay just out of sight of the bird and repeat the phrase you want it to learn, for at least fifteen minutes every morning and evening.
    III. It is important to leave the bird without any words of encouragement or farewell; otherwise it might combine stray remarks or phrases, such as "Good night," with the phrase you are trying to teach it.
    IV. For this reason, to train your bird to imitate your words you should keep it free of any distractions, especially other noises, while you are giving it "lesson."
    V. After your repetition, you should quietly leave the bird alone for a while, to think over what it has just heard.
    The BEST order is:
     A. I, IV, II, V, III   B. I, II, IV, III, V   C. III, II, I, V, IV   D. III, I, V, IV, II

25. I. As a school approaches, fishermen from neighboring communities join their fishing boats together as a fleet, and string their gill nets together to make a huge fence that is held up by cork floats.
    II. At a signal from the party leaders, or *nakura*, the family members pound the sides of the boats or beat the water with long poles, creating a sudden and deafening noise.
    III. The fishermen work together to drag the trap into a half-circle that may reach 300 yards in diameter, and then the families move their boats to form the other half of the circle around the school of fish.
    IV. The school of fish flee from the commotion into the awaiting trap, where a final wall of net is thrown over the open end of the half-circle, securing the day's haul.
    V. Indonesian people from the area around the Sulu islands live on the sea, in floating villages made of lashed-together or stilted homes, and make much of their living by fishing their home waters for migrating schools of snapper, scad, and other fish.
    The BEST order is:
     A. I, V, III, IV, II   B. I, II, IV, III, V   C. V, I, II, III, IV   D. V, I, III, II, IV

KEY (CORRECT ANSWERS)

1.	D		11.	C
2.	D		12.	A
3.	B		13.	D
4.	A		14.	C
5.	C		15.	D
6.	C		16.	C
7.	D		17.	A
8.	D		18.	D
9.	A		19.	B
10.	B		20.	A

21.	A
22.	C
23.	B
24.	A
25.	D

BIOLOGY-BACTERIOLOGY

The science of biology is concerned with the study of living organisms, their habits, food requirements, and general functions. Among the myriad types of living organisms which inhabit this planet, the bacteria form a very important part. The study of biology and of bacteriology is of basic importance since these sciences are the foundations upon which sanitation and sewage treatment are based. Without knowledge of the fundamental factors concerning these living organisms and their relation to one another and to human beings it would be difficult to understand the principles upon which all treatment processes are based.

BACTERIOLOGY

Bacteria are minute living organisms, each consisting of a single cell. These organisms are so small that they can be seen only when magnified under a microscope. Thus they are included in the term microorganisms. Food assimilation, waste excretion, respiration, growth and all other activities are carried on through the action of the one single cell. Many bacteria have characteristics ordinarily associated with the animal kingdom and others generally applied to the plant kingdom. In some respects, they form a link between these two types of living organisms. There are many different kinds of bacteria, varying widely in size, shape and function.

The cells of the bacteria consist of an outer shell or membrane, an inner jelly-like material called protoplasm, and a nucleus within the protoplasm of the cell. As with all other living organisms, bacteria can reproduce, but they do this by a process known as fission. The adult cell constricts in the middle, the constriction increases until finally the cell divides into two smaller cells, each a complete living organism. These two daughter cells grow and in turn divide to continue the process. It is estimated that the average bacterium will divide at intervals of 20-30 minutes. Thus, the increase in the number of bacteria under favorable conditions is tremendous in a short period of time, such as 12 hours, if all the daughter cells were to survive. (Figure 29).

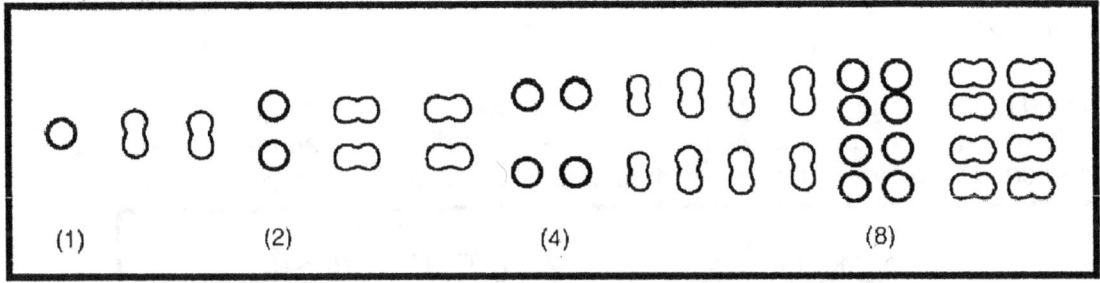

FIGURE 1 - REPRODUCTION OF BACTERIA

Bacteria are found everywhere in our environment. They are present in the soil, and thru the agency of dust they are suspended in the air. They are found in water as the result of passage of rain through the air and the various water sources flowing through and over the ground. Bacteria are present in the bodies of all living organisms and many of them carry on very useful and necessary functions related to the life of the larger organism.

Bacilli are rod-shaped cells, some longer or shorter than others with the different kinds also varying in width. A single rod-shaped cell is called a bacillus.

Cocci appear as round or spherial cells. Some occur as pairs and are called diplococci, others as chain and are designated as *streptococci*, still others are arranged in irregular shaped groups and are called *staphylococci*.

Other bacteria have different shapes, such as a comma or crescent, others are spiral. Each is designated by a special name but the bacilli and cocci are the most common.

Flagella are hair-like projections from the shell of a microorganism. Movement of these flagella provide a means of locomotion for the cell which can then move in its environment, a process generally ascribed to an animal. Not all bacteria have this property and as such, are more nearly like plants.

Saprophytes are bacteria that can carry on an independent existence finding their own food supply adapting themselves to the conditions of their environment and carrying on their work without stimulus from other organisms.

The saprophytic bacteria, in general, obtain their food from dead organic matter which they attack and decompose or break down into simpler substances. Thus, they can obtain the food supply that is necessary for their continued growth, while at the same time carrying on the very useful function of destroying the dead matter. Without the action of the saprophytic bacteria, it would be impossible for other organisms to live on this planet since there would be no way to dispose of the dead organisms which would eventually cover the earth preventing growth of plants and the carrying on of natural functions essential for living organisms. Saprophytic bacteria break down the complex organic components of matter through the process known as decay or decomposition into simpler substances. These, in turn, serve as a food supply for plants, which become a food supply for animals, and the cycle of life is continued without the loss of matter. As an illustration of the changes in dead organic matter that are brought about by the activity of the bacteria, we might consider the natural process of decay and decomposition of organic compounds containing nitrogen, as shown by the nitrogen cycle. (Figure 30)

All living matter contains nitrogen bound with carbon, oxygen, hydrogen and other elements to form organic molecules. When these organisms die, the dead material is immediately a source of food for the saprophytic bacteria, which change these complex organic

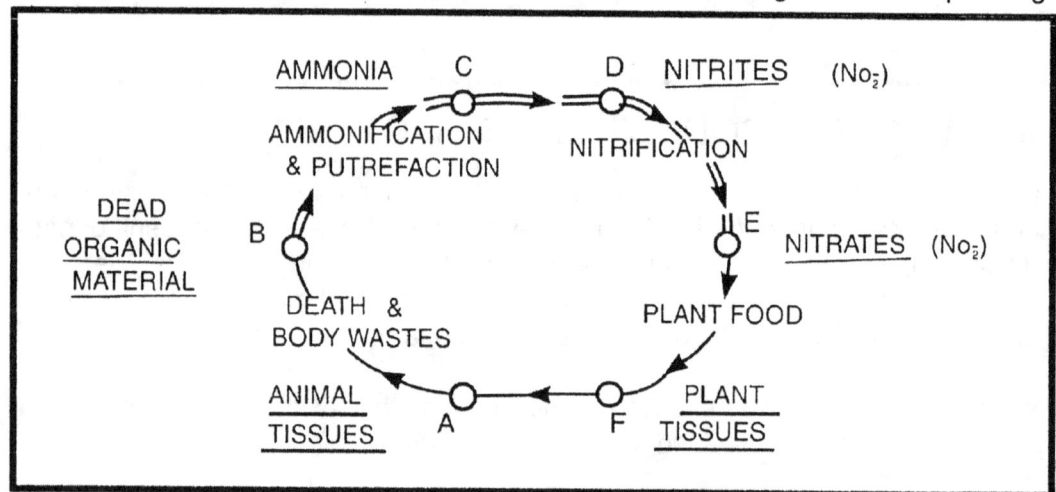

FIGURE 2 - THE NITROGEN CYCLE

molecules to simpler forms of nitrogenous matter, thence to ammonia, then to nitrites, and then to nitrates. The nitrates are the end product and the simplest and most useful form in which nitrogen exists. The nitrates are the basis of fertilizers and serve as a food for plants, which grow and become the food for living animals, which in turn grow until finally they die, and the cycle is completed and continues on and on. Thus, there is no loss of matter and complete usage is made of all of the elements composing living matter. In a similar manner, organic compounds containing sulfur, phosphorous, carbon and other chemical elements are decomposed through serving as a food supply for saprophytic bacteria.

Parasites, as contrasted to the saprophytic organisms, are bacteria that cannot live an independent existence, cannot find their own food supply, but must remain in close association with some other living organisms, from which they can obtain food already prepared. Parasites are dependent on the body of the host organisms to secure the environmental conditions upon which their existence and growth depend. They, however, carry on a similar type of decay and decomposition of this food supply, producing as a result end products which are necessary for the nourishment of the host. Most of these parasitic bacteria are beneficient and are necessary for the proper functioning of the living organism with which they are associated.

Pathogens. Among the parasitic bacteria are some which produce end products of their growth that are poisonous to the host organism and which produce a condition that is called disease. Some of them are pathogenic only to human beings in that they produce disease only in the body of human beings. Others are pathogenic to certain types of warm-blooded animals and some are pathogenic only to plants. There are a few types of saprophytic bacteria which have all of the characteristics of that class but which can, if they find entry into the body of an animal, produce end products which cause disease, such as anthrax or tetanus, in the body of the invaded animal. These particular saprophytic bacteria are also termed pathogenic.

Bacterial Growth. All bacteria require food for their continued life and growth and all are affected by the conditions of their environment. Like human beings, they consume food, they respire, they need moisture, they require heat, and they give off waste products. Their food requirements are very definite and have been, in general, already outlined. Without an adequate food supply of the type the specific organism requires, bacteria will not grow and multiply at their maximum rate and they will, therefore, not perform their full and complete functions.

Aerobic Bacteria. All bacteria require oxygen for their growth processes. Some require oxygen in its elementary gaseous form, which they obtain from the air. Such bacteria are designated as aerobic.

Anaerobic Bacteria. Some bacteria cannot live in the presence of free gaseous oxygen, but must obtain the oxygen needed for their respiration by decomposing or breaking down complex substances. These bacteria are designated as anaerobic.

Facultative Bacteria. There is a third type of bacteria which, though normally aerobic, can accustom itself to living in the absence of free gaseous oxygen or which, though normally anaerobic, can accustom itself to living in the presence of free gaseous oxygen. These are termed facultative bacteria.

Temperature Requirements. Bacteria are very sensitive to heat. Some live best at ordinary outdoor temperatures, varying from 60° to 68° F. Some, particularly the parasitic forms, require higher temperatures, approximately that of the body of living animals, 98° F. Some can live only at very cold temperatures, just above the freezing point of water. Any marked change from the optimum temperature requirements of specific bacteria causes a reduction in the activities of the bacteria, and if severe enough, may cause their death. If the temperature of the environment is raised to the boiling point of water, nearly all types of bacteria are destroyed.

Moisture Requirements. Bacteria require a moist environment for their most effective activities. If removed from such an environment for any length of time and drying takes place, most bacterial cells are destroyed. Under the most optimum environmental conditions of temperature, moisture, food supply and oxygen, the bacteria will multiply and grow at their maximum rate, producing their maximum amount of work. Any changes in the environmental conditions will cause an immediate decrease in the rate of growth, and possibly the death and destruction of the living forms.

Spore Formation. Some bacteria particularly those of the saprophytic type, when obliged to live in a very unfavorable environment with an inadequate food supply for any length of time, develop into a resistant form called a spore or seed. These spores are not affected by the environment, no food is required for their existence, and no growth results. A nucleus of life, however, is maintained and when the spore is again placed in a favorable environment it will sprout or develop into an active cell again. Parasitic bacteria, in general, do not form spores while saprophytes frequently do.

NORMAL CHARACTERISTICS OF SAPROPHYTIC AND PARASITIC BACTERIA

	Saprophytes	*Parasites*
Optimum temperature	Atmospheric	Body
Normal food material	Dead organic	Living
Oxygen requirements	Aerobic and anaerobic	Most anaerobic
Spore formation	Usually	Seldom
Effect on animals	Mostly non-pathogenic	Pathogenic and non-pathogenic

Mutual Activities. In the process of growth all bacteria produce waste products just as all other organisms do, and if these waste products were allowed to accumulate, they would destroy the particular form which produced them. However, other types of bacteria may find these waste products a satisfactory food supply, grow in their presence, and carry decomposition of the organic matter a step further until in turn their food supply is exhausted or their waste products accumulate to a sufficient degree to cause their destruction. Thus, the decay of organic matter is continuously carried on by many different types of bacteria, each of which carries the process of chemical decomposition forward. This is essentially what occurs in familiar process of sewage solids digestion. When the food supply is plentiful it is possible for two or more varieties of bacteria to exist side by side provided that the waste production of one strain is not toxic for the other. If the food supply lessens, or if waste products produced by one strain are toxic to other strains, the phenomena known as overgrowth may appear. This is a condition where one strain of organism may predominate to the exclusion of all others. Eventually however, waste products of the metabolism of the organism, unless they are removed, will become deleterious to the organism itself and the number of cells in a culture will decrease.

Toxic Agents. Living bacteria are sensitive not only to changes in the environment but can readily be poisoned or destroyed by many chemical substances. Such things as large concentrations of salt will destroy certain types of bacteria and this process has been used for many centuries to preserve such dead organic matter as meat or fish. Others are destroyed by strong acids or strong alkalis and by the addition to the environment of such chemical substances as chlorine, iodine or bromine. The destructive action of chemicals is a time-concentration effect. Thus, a low concentration will kill when present in the environment for a long period of time and a large concentration will kill in a short time.

WATER BIOLOGY

Bacteria. Bacteria are so widely distributed in nature that it is not surprising that all natural waters contain a fairly large variety. Some of these are saprophytic bacteria leached from the soil, others may be parasitic. Even pathogenic bacteria may be present in the water through contamination by waste matter of human or animal origin. Any water supply contaminated by sewage is certain to contain a bacterial group called "coliform." This is a group comprising more than 20 individual strains and termed coliform because of the fact that they have their natural habitat in the large intestine of human beings and animals. These bacteria are not usually pathogenic. The presence of pathogenic bacteria in water, as a result of contamination by sewage, is dependent upon an individual contributing to that sewage being ill of an intestinal disease and upon the survival of the pathogen in an environment which is not favorable to it. Coliform bacteria, on the other hand, are always present if sewage is present and are, generally much more hardy than pathogens. It is for this reason that the bacteriologic evaluation of water is always based upon a bacteriologic analysis to determine if coliform bacteria are present and in what concentration.

PLANKTON

In addition to bacteria other living organisms are commonly found in water and sewage. These are plankton. They are higher in the life scale than bacteria. They range in size from minute one-cell organisms only slightly larger than bacteria to much larger forms easily visible to the unaided eye. Some are plants, other are animals; some are capable of independent motion while others are not. Some idea of the complexity of size, shape, and metabolism of plankton may be gained by consideration of some characteristics of the most important groups of organisms included under that designation.

Algae. This is a very large group of plant forms distinguished by the fact that they contain chlorophyl—the green coloring matter of plants. Under favorable conditions they grow prolifically in water and sewage and heavy growths are easily detected by the presence of green-colored scum or "bloom." Under the influence of sunlight, chlorophyl-bearing plants absorb carbon dioxide and evolve oxygen. Pond waters which have heavy growths of algae frequently are saturated with oxygen during the daylight hours although the oxygen level decreases as darkness advances. Using water, carbon dioxide, and mineral matter secured from the environment, algae synthesize the complex proteins, fats, and cellulose constituents which made up their cell structure. The growth of algae is stimulated by the presence of nitrogen and phosphorous salts and also to some extent by calcium and magnesium salts. Growths in hard water are therefore usually heavier than in soft waters. Some algae are very tiny and have a single cell structure, other are multicellular and grow in a variety of forms, including branching plant-like structures hundreds of feet long. Many have pigments other than chlorophyl so that the actual color may be green, blue-green, or even red or brown. They are found most often in relatively pure water although not exclusively so. Some of the blue-green varieties are capable of growing quite well in heavily polluted water and even in sewage.

Fungi. Fungi are also plants, but in contract to the algae they do not contain chlorophyl. They are filamentous type organisms. For the purposes of simplicity, when we speak of sewage fungi we include filamentous bacteria and filamentous algae although, strictly speaking, these latter are not fungi. Fungi are commonly found in water and sewage and in the latter they are often observed growing in gray-colored cottony masses which attach themselves to the walls and structures in sewage treatment units. A common organism of this type is known as sphaerotilus. Fungi masses frequently clog the pipes and screens in the sewage plant and reduce the flow in channels. Their metabolism is dependent upon the availability of oxygen and a plentiful supply of organic matter.

Protozoa. Animals coming under the heading of plankton include, among other forms, protozoa. These are generally considered to be higher forms of life than the algae. They are frequently motile and are usually associated with sewage pollution. There are very many varieties and most of them feed on other microscopic organisms, primarily bacteria. They are frequently found growing in large masses as well as individual cells suspended in the water. There are thousands of varieties ranging in size from submicroscopic to macroscopic.

Crustaceae. These are small animals ranging in size from 0.2 to 0.3 millimeter long which move very rapidly through the water in search of food. They have recognizable head and posterior sections. They form a principal source of food for small fish and are found largely in relatively fresh natural water.

Rotifera. These are tiny animal forms which are characterized by the presence of cilia-short hair-like appendages which serve the double purpose of providing locomotion and creating a current in the water so that food will be drawn to the organism. Rotifera feed on decomposing organic matter and are found in bodies of water where such matter is present.

Worms. Flat worms or nematodes are varieties of worms which may be found in water and in sewage. Flat worms feed principally on algae and are found in the lower depths of ponds because they dislike and avoid light. They range in size from the fraction of a millimeter to several centimeters. Nematodes are parasitic worms living on other organisms, including man. It is believed that those which are parasitic in man are usually associated with contaminated food rather than contaminated water. Nematodes are very hardy and will survive over wide variations in temperature and humidity. They even survive under prolonged drying. They are very abundant in sewage sludge and are believed to play an important part in the stabilization of sludge.

Water Borne Disease. Pathogenic bacteria, which cause certain diseases, when discharged into water, can survive and be transferred through the agency of the water from one person to another. Among these so-called water-borne diseases are typhoid fever, dysentery, cholera, and various types of diarrheal ailments designated as gastro enteritis. Thus, the presence of these organisms in water causes a contamination of the water and renders it both unfit and unsafe for consumption. People who drink the water containing these particular pathogenic bacteria can readily acquire the corresponding disease in this way.

Safe Water. Obviously, then, the removal of bacteria is a necessary step in making water suitable for human consumption. Another necessary step is to prevent these pathogenic bacteria from getting into a water supply. Only water free from pathogenic bacteria can be considered of safe and satisfactory quality.

Laboratory Control. To determine if water is safe or if our precautionary methods are eliminating waste, and thus pathogenic bacteria from water, it is necessary that some means be devised for detecting the number of bacteria in water. To actually detect such pathogenic bacteria as those causing typhoid fever, dysentery, or other water-borne diseases is a very laborious, time-consuming process. Contrary to the opinion of most people, such examinations of water are not made. Rather, it is desirable to determine whether polluting material in the form of waste products from living animals has entered the water and to prevent further contamination from this means, or to remove the bacteria from water which has already received this type of polluting material. The procedure used is to determine the presence of an organism indicative of contamination of a water supply by the waste products from the intestinal discharges of warm-blooded animals.

Coliform organism. All warm-blooded animals harbor in their intestinal tract parasitic bacteria of various types. All members of this one specific group are designated as the coliform group of bacteria. These microorganisms are not normally pathogenic and function in the digestive processes of the host organism. They are discharged from the intestinal tract in tremendous numbers. They will always be present in large numbers in sewage, which usually contains at least 4,000,000 to 5,000,000 coliform bacteria per ml. If sewage enters a water, the bacteria are carried with it and will survive there for long periods of time. Thus, their presence provides positive evidence of pollution and the possible presence of the pathogenic bacteria from the discharges of the animal bodies. Their detection by laboratory examination is relatively simple.

Index of Pollution. The number of these bacteria that are present in any definite volume of water is a measure of the amount of sewage or waste which has been discharged into that water, and can be interpreted as a measure of the safety of the water for human consumption. If large numbers of these bacteria are present, there will be a large amount of pollution and the water is unsatisfactory and potentially unsafe. A smaller number of these microorganisms, of course, shows a lesser concentration of pollution. A very few coliform bacteria, less than one per 100 ml of water, indicates that the amount of pollution is too small to present a definite hazard and that it can be considered of safe quality.

GLOSSARY OF BACTERIOLOGICAL TERMS

Contents

		Page
ACID-FAST BACTERIA	AMYLASE	1
ANAEROBES	ATTENUATED	2
AUTOCLAVE	BY-PRODUCTS	3
CAPSULE	COLUMELLA	4
COMMENSALISM	DIFFUSE NUCLEI	5
DIPLOID NUCLEUS	EXTRACELLULAR ENZYMES	6
FACULTATIVELY ANAEROBIC	HAPLOID NUCLEUS	7
HUMUS	INTRACELLULAR ENZYMES	8
INTRAMOLECULAR RESPIRATION	METABIOSIS	9
METABOLISM	MYCELIUM	10
NATURAL IMMUNITY	PARASITES	11
PASSIVE IMMUNITY	PLASMOLYSIS	12
PLEOMORPHISM	REFLECTED LIGHT	13
RENNIN	SEWERAGE	14
SLIME LAYER	STRICK PARASITES	15
STRINGY MILK	TOXOID	16
TRANSMITTED LIGHT	WINOGRADSKY TEST	17
YEAST	ZYGOTE	18

GLOSSARY OF BACTERIOLOGICAL TERMS

<u>A</u>

ACID-FAST BACTERIA
   Bacteria that strongly resist decoloration with acid-alcohol after being stained with a hot dye such as carbol fuchsin. *Mycobacterium tuberculosis* is a typical example.

ACQUIRED IMMUNITY
   Immunity that an individual obtains after a period of natural susceptibility.

ACTIVATED SLUDGE PROCESS
   A method of sewage purification in which a little "ripe" sewage is added to the fresh sewage to be treated, which is then submitted to extensive aeration.

ACTIVE IMMUNITY
   Immunity in which the immunizing agent is produced by the metabolism of the immunized individual.

AEROBES
   Organisms that can grow in the presence of air.

AGAR
   1. A polysaccharide material extracted from sea weeds.
   2. A common term applied to a culture medium solidified with this material, such as nutrient agar.

AGGLUTINATION
   The clumping together of bacteria through the action of agglu-tinins homologous with them.

AGGLUTININS
   A kind of antibody that causes the clumping together of the corresponding antigen particles, such as bacterial bodies.

ALGAE
   Thallophytic plants that carry on photosynthesis with the aid of chlorophyll or other pigment.

ALLERGY
   A state of hypersentivity to a foreign substance such as protein.

AMMONIFICATION
   The formation of ammonia from organic compounds.

AMPHITRICHIC
   With a tuft of flagella at each end of the cell. Resulting from cell division but not separation of two sister cells each carrying flagella at one end. Terminal flagellation.

AMYLASE
   The enzyme that hydrolyzes starch to maltose. Diastase. Ptyalin.

ANAEROBES
Organisms that cannot grow in the presence of air.

ANAPHYLACTIC SHOCK
The response of the body to the injection of a substance to which the body is abnormally sensitive.

ANAPHYLAXIS
A state of hypersensitiveness to a foreign protein or other substance, brought about by an initial injection of the substance.

ANOREXIA
Loss of appetite.

ANTAGONISM
A relationship between species of microorganisms in which one kills or injures the other. Antibiosis.

ANTIBIOTIC
A substance produced by a living organism which will inhibit or destroy other forms of life, expecially pathogenic microorganisms. Examples are penicillin, streptomycin, bacitracin, etc.

ANTIBODY
A substance produced by the body under the stimulus of an antigen and capable of reacting with it *in vitro*.

ANTIGEN
A substance, usually a foreign protein, that, if injected into the body, stimulates the production of an antibody such as antitoxin.

ANTISEPTIC
A chemical substance that, in the strength used, will inhibit the activities of microorganisms without killing them.

ANTITOXIN
An antibody that has the power of neutralizing the effects of the homologous toxin that served as an antigen for its production.

ASCOSPORES
Spores produced in definite numbers, usually eight, by free cell formation within a sac or ascus.

ASCUS
The spore-bearing sac of the *Ascomycetes*.

ATTENUATED
Made weaker than normal, or less pathogenic.

AUTOCLAVE
An apparatus used for heating materials under steam pressure. Similar in principle to a pressure cooker.

AUTOLYSIS
Self-digestion due to the action of enzymes upon the tissues that produced them, as the over-ripening of bananas and other kinds of fruit, or the breakdown of dead bacterial cells.

AUTOTROPHIC BACTERIA
Bacteria that can live without a supply of organic matter, and can obtain energy from inorganic materials, or in some instances from sunlight.

B

BACTEREMIA
The presence of bacteria in the blood stream. Septicemia.

BACTERIOLYSIS
The disintegration of bacterial cells.

BACTERIOPHAGE
A specific virus capable of destroying living bacteria.

BALLISTOSPORES
Asexual spores formed by yeasts of the family *Sporobolo-mycetaceae*. They arise on sterigmata and are shot off by a drop excretion mechanism.

BARRIERS OF INFECTION
Mechanical obstructions, such as skin and mucous membranes, that prevent pathogenic organisms from reaching a vulnerable region.

BROWNIAN MOVEMENT
The movement of visible particles by the bombardment of molecules of the suspending fluid.

BUDDING
A method of cell division in which a small area of the cell wall softens and protoplasm including a nucleus is forced out and is later cut off by constriction, thus forming a new cell.

BUTTER CULTURE
A pure culture or a definite mixture of bacterial species added to cream after pasteurization to give desired flavor and consistency to the butter made from it.

BY-PRODUCTS
Substances that remain after certain elements have been removed for use by the organism, e.g., nitrites, after oxygen has been removed from nitrates.

C

CAPSULE
A thickened slime layer of carbohydrate material surrounding the cell wall of many species of bacteria.

CARBOHYDRASES
The group of enzymes that hydrolyze complex carbohydrates to simpler ones. The amylolytic group.

CARRIER OF DISEASE
A person or animal that harbors the organisms of disease without showing symptoms.

CATEGORIES
The several group names order, families, genera, etc., used for classifying living things.

CELLULASE
The enzyme that hydrolyzes cellulose into cellobiose.

CHEMOSYNTHESIS
The obtaining of energy by the oxidation of inorganic substances, followed by its use for the building of organic compounds.

CHEMOTAXIS
The ability of organisms to respond to chemical stimuli by moving toward or away from the region of greatest concentration.

CHLAMYDOSPORES
Thick-walled spores formed by a rounding up of cells of a mycelium.

CHROMOGENESIS
The production of pigment.

COCCI
Bacterial that are spherical or nearly so.

COLIFORM GROUP
All aerobic and facultatively anerobic gram negative non-spore forming rods which ferment lactose with gas formation.

COLIPHAGE
A specific bacteriophage that is capable of destroying Escherichia coli.

COLONY
A visible collection of bacteria resulting from the multiplication and growth of a single individual.

COLUMELLA
A dome-shaped, non-sporeforming structure extending upward from the sporangiophore into the base of a sporangium, as in Rhizopus.

COMMENSALISM
A relationship between species of organisms in which one receives benefit and the other neither benefit nor harm. Metabiosis.

COMPLEMENT
A thermolabel, non-specific constituent of the normal blood of man aiding in the destruction of all kinds of bacteria.

CONDENSER
A large lens beneath the stage of a microscope, for concentrating light on the object from below.

CONIDIA
Fungus spores cut off from the tips of hyphae by construction.

CONIDIOPHORE
A stalk arising from the vegetative mycelium and supporting sterigmata that produce one or more conidia.

CONJUGATION
The union of two gamete cells in sexual reproduction.

CONSTRICTION
A method of cell division in which the cell is cut in two by a circular furrow surrounding it.

D

DARK-FIELD ILLUMINATION
A method of illuminating objects for microscopic examination whereby the object is made to appear luminous against a dark background.

DECAY
The destruction of organic materials through the action of enzymes produced by microorganisms.

DEHYDROGENASES
A group of enzymes that remove hydrogen from compounds and thus produce the effect of oxidation.

DENITRIFICATION
The formation of free nitrogen of nitrous oxide from nitrates.

DICK TEST
A skin test to determine whether a person is susceptible to scarlet fever.

DIFFUSE NUCLEI
Nuclei composed of chromatin material scattered throughout the cytoplasm rather than enclosed within a nuclear membrane.

DIPLOID NUCLEUS
A neucleus having a complete number of paired chromosomes for the species. See HAPLOID.

DISINFECTANTS
Chemical substances capable of killing pathogenic microorganisms.

E

EFFLUENT
Partially or completely treated sewage flowing out of any sewage treatment device.

ELECTRON MICROSCOPE
A microscope similar in principle to the compound light microscope but which uses electrons instead of light as a source of radiation.

ENDOENZYMES
Same as intracellular enzymes.

ENDOTOXINS
Toxins that remain within the cells that produce them and do not stimulate the production of corresponding antitoxins.

ENVIRONMENT
The composite of all conditions surrounding an organism.

ENZYME
A biological catalyst.

EPIDEMIOLOGY
The science of tracing the sources from which diseases spread.

ETIOLOGY
The science of causes, e.g., causes of disease.

EXCRETIONS
Substances that have become so changed in composition through metabolism that they are no longer useful to the organism that produced them and are cast off, e.g., carbon dioxide.

EXOENZYMES
Same as EXTRACELLULAR ENZYMES.

EXOTOXINS
Toxins that diffuse from the cells that produce them into the surrounding medium. They are antigenic and stimulate the formation of antitoxins.

EXTRACELLULAR ENZYMES
Enzymes that diffuse out of the cells that formed them.

F

FACULTATIVELY ANAEROBIC
Organisms that can grow in either the presence or absence of air.

FACULTATIVELY PARASITIC
Organisms that can live either as parasites or as saprophytes.

FALSE BRANCHING
A kind of branching of filaments in which the cells do not branch, but the branch of the filament is held to the main filament by a common sheath surrounding both.

FERMENTATION
A process carried on by microorganisms whereby organic materials, usually carbohydrates, are decomposed with the formation of acids and sometimes carbon dioxide and alcohol.

FISSION
A method of cell division by constriction in which two daughter cells of equal size are formed.

FLAGELLA
Slender protoplasmic strands that extend from the cell and serve as organs of locomotion.

FUNGI IMPERFECTI
A heterogeneous group of fungi that have no sexual stage. Apparently most of them are degenerate *Asoomycetes*.

FUNGUS
A thallophytic plant that lacks chlorophyll and is of filmentous structure.

G

GAMETES
Two haploid cells that unite in sexual reproduction.

GENOTYPE
The sum total of the determinants controlling the reaction range of an individual or a cell.

GROWTH
1. Increase in size of an individual.
2. Increase in numbers of microorganisms.
3. A visible mass of microorganisms formed by reproduction and enlargement.

H

HANGING DROP
A drop of liquid suspended for study from the under side of a cover glass mounted on a slide with a depression in the surface.

HAPLOID NUCLEUS
A nucleus having a complete number of single chromosomes for the species. See DIPLOID.

HUMUS
Organic matter decomposed to such an extent that its original structure is no longer recognizable.

HYDROLASES
Enzymes that bring about chemical change by the addition of water that goes into chemical union with the substance acted upon.

HYPERSENSITIVITY
An abnormally high degree of sensitiveness to foreign substances such as proteins.

HYPERTROPHY
An abnormal multiplication of cells resulting in the formation of nodules, tumors, etc.

HYPHAE
Branches of a fungus mycelium.

I

IMHOFF TANK
A specially constructed septic tank having a flow chamber above and a sludge chamber below.

IMMUNITY
The ability of an animal or plant to resist disease even when the pathogenic organisms or their products reach a vulnerable region.

IMPRESSED VARIATION
A kind of variation brought about by some recognizably unfavorable condition.

INFLAMMATION
A morbid condition characterized by swelling, redness, and pain, usually in a localized region.

INFLUENT
Sewage, treated or partially treated, flowing into any sewage treatment device.

INOCULUM
Material containing microorganisms and used for the inoculation of media or hosts.

INTERMITTENT STERILIZATION
A sterilization process involving the heating of the material to a temperature of 80-100 C. for a time up to an hour on each of three successive days. Fractional sterilization. Tyndal-lization.

INTERMOLECULAR RESPIRATION
A form of respiration in which oxygen is taken from one kind of molecule and used to oxidize another.

INTRACELLULAR ENZYMES
Enzymes that remain within the cells that produced them. Endoenzymes.

INTRAMOLECULAR RESPIRATION
A form of respiration in which there is a rearrangement of atoms within the molecule resulting in a release of energy.

INVOLUTION FORMS
Cells of microorganisms large in size and of unusual form. Generally considered abnormal.

IRON BACTERIA
Bacteria that contain ferric hydroxide in the stalk or the sheath.

IRRITABILITY
The capacity of an organism for response to change in the environment.

L

LENS
A piece of glass or other transparent substance used for magnifying or reducing the apparent size of objects.

LIPOLYTIC ENZYMES
Enzymes that hydrolyze fats into fatty acids and glycerol.

LOPHOTRICHIC
With flagella in a tuft at one end of the cell. Terminal flagellation.

LYOPHILIZE
To dry a protein, usually from the frozen state, in such a way so it is still soluble. As applied to microorganisms it involves the freezing and drying of the organisms so that many of the cells will remain viable for long periods of time.

LYSIN
An enzyme or other substance that breaks down or dissolves organic substances.

M

MANTOUX TEST
A tuberculin test in which the tuberculin is injected in-tradermally.

MASS MORPHOLOGY
The morphology of bacterial groups, colonies, etc., as contrasted with individual cells.

MECHANISM OF INFECTION
The means by which microorganisms produce disease.

MESOPHILES
Bacteria that grow best at moderate temperatures, having an optimum of 25° C. to 45° C.

METABIOSIS
Same as COMMENSALISM.

METABOLISM
Any chemical change brought about by a living thing in its use of food.

MICROAEROPHILIC
Organisms that require free oxygen of less concentration than that found in the atmosphere.

MICROMANIPULATOR
A complicated piece of apparatus used for fine dissection under the microscope, or for single cell isolation.

MICRON
A unit of measurement having a value of 0.001 of a millimeter.

MICROORGANISMS
Forms of life that are microscopic in size, or nearly so.

MICROPHILES
Bacteria having a narrow temperature range for growth.

MILLIMICRON
0.001 micron or 0.000001 mm. A unit of measurement often used in designating the size of virus particles.

MITOSIS
Division of a cell with a diploid nucleus in which all of the chromosomes divide, resulting in two diploid daughter cells.

MOLD
A saprophytic fungus that is of simple filamentous structure.

MONOTRICHIC
With a flagellum occurring at one end of the cell. Terminal flagellation.

MORBIDITY
The frequency of occurrence of cases of a disease.

MORPHOLOGY
That branch of biological science that deals with qualities that appear to the eye size, form, color, etc.

MORTALITY
The percentage of deaths among those afflicted with a disease.

MUTATION
A change from some parental character occurring in the offspring. More permanent than variation.

MYCELIUM
The branching, thread-like structure that makes up the vegetative body of a fungus.

N

NATURAL IMMUNITY
Immunity that an individual possesses by virtue of its race or species. Immunity present from the beginning of life of the individual.

NECROSIS
The death of tissues.

NITRATE REDUCTION
The formation of nitrites or ammonia from nitrates.

NITRIFICATION
The formation of nitric acid or nitrates from ammonia.

NITROGEN FIXATION
The formation of nitrogen compounds from free nitrogen.

NON-SYMBIOTIC NITROGEN FIXATION
Fixation of nitrogen by organisms living independently, as *Azotobacter* and *Clostridium*.

NOSEPIECE
The portion of a microscope into which the objectives are screwed.

O

OBJECTIVE
The system of lenses in a compound microscope that is used next to the object to be studied.

OCULAR
The combination of lenses at the top of a compound microscope. Also called an eyepiece.

OIDIA
Thin walled spores formed by the separation of undifferentiated cells of a mycelium.

OPSONINS
Antibodies which make bacteria more readily ingested by phagocytes.

OSMOSIS
The tendency of fluids to pass through a membrane that separates two portions of different concentration.

P

PARASITES
Organisms that obtain their food from the living substance of other organisms.

PASSIVE IMMUNITY
Immunity in which the immunized individual does not produce its own immunizing agent but receives it from one with active immunity.

PASTEURIZATION
Heating at a temperature that will kill most objectionable microorganisms, excepting spore-forming bacteria and ther-mophiles.

PATHOGENICITY
The ability to produce disease.

PATHOGENS
Organisms that cause disease in other forms of life.

PATHOLOGY
A study of the abnormal conditions that occur in the tissues as a result of disease.

PERITRICHIC
With flagella distributed all over the cell body. Lateral flagellation.

PHAGOCYTES
Leucocytes or other living cells that have the power of ingesting bacteria.

PHENOL COEFFICIENT
The killing strength of a disinfectant, relative to that of phenol.

PHOTOGENESIS
The production of light. Phosphorescence.

PHOTOSYNTHESIS
The formation of carbohydrates from simpler food materials, using light as the source of energy.

PHYSIOLOGY
That branch of biological science which deals with the functions and activities of living things nutrition, growth, reproduction, irritiability, etc.

PLAQUES
Clear zones in streaks of bacterial growth resulting from the lysis of bacteria by bacteriophage.

PLANE OF DIVISION
The direction in which a cleavage furrow divides a cell.

PLASMODESMID
A protoplasmic strand extending from one bacterial cell to another.

PLASMOLYSIS
The shrinkage of cell contents through the withdrawal of water by osmotic action.

PLEOMORPHISM
Exhibiting several forms or shapes. Polymorphism.

PLEUROPNEUMONIA GROUP
Microorganisms that grow in cell-free culture media with the development of polymorphic structures as rings, globules, filaments, and minute reproductive bodies.

POLYMORPHISM
Exhibiting several forms or shapes. Pleomorphism.

PORTALS OF INFECTION
Openings through which pathogenic organisms pass into the body of the host.

POST-FISSION MOVEMENTS
Movements of cells following fission, whereby the two adjacent cells are finally separated.

PRECIPITINS
A kind of antibody that forms a precipitate with an antigen that was previously in solution.

PROCESSING
Preliminary treatment, canning, and sterilization of foods. The term is often used for a single one of these operations such as sterilization.

PROTEOLYSIS
The destruction of proteins by enzymes.

PROTEOLYTIC ENZYMES
Enzymes that hydrolze proteins and related compounds.

PROTOZOA
Unicellular members of the animal kingdom.

PSYCHROPHILES
Bacteria that grow best at relatively low temperatures, having an optimum of 15 C to 20 C.

PUTREFACTION
The chemical decomposition of proteins and related compounds, usually with the production of disagreeable odors.

R

R-COLONIES
Colonies that have a rough surface, although belonging to a species that usually produces smooth colonies.

REFLECTED LIGHT
Light that strikes the surface of an object being studied with a microscope and is reflected back into the lens.

RENNIN
The enzyme that changes the soluble casein of milk into the solid paracasein in the presence of calcium.

RESOLVING POWER
The ability of a lens to reveal fine detail. It is measured in terms of the least distance between two points at which they can be identified as two rather than as a single blurred object.

RESPIRATION
Any chemical reaction whereby energy is released for life processes.

RICKETTSIAE
Microorganisms that are obligate intracellular parasites or that are dependent directly on living cells. They are not ultramicroscopic but are adapted to intracellular life in arthropod tissue.

ROPY MILK
Milk that is viscid because of the presence of capsule-forming bacteria such as *Alcaligenes viscosus*.

S

SAPROPHYTES
Organisms that use non-living organic matter for food.

SCHICK TEST
A skin test to determine whether a person is susceptible to diphtheria. Similar to the Dick test for scarlet fever.

S-COLONIES
Colonies that have a smooth surface, although belong to a species that may produce rough-surfaced colonies.

SECONDARY INVADERS
Saprophytic organisms that invade the body of a host in the wake of a pathogenic species.

SECRETIONS
Substances that serve a useful purpose to the organisms that produce them, e.g., enzymes.

SEPTATE MYCELIUM
A mycelium subdivided into cells by cross-walls or septa.

SEPTIC TANK
A deep vat or chamber used for the anaerobic treatment of sewage.

SEPTICEMIA
The presence of bacteria in the blood stream. Bacteremia.

SEWERAGE
The system employed for the handling of sewage.

SLIME LAYER
A carbohydrate layer surrounding all bacterial cells which, if it becomes extensive, is called a capsule.

SLUDGE
The mass of solids remaining after a sewage treating process is completed or wet sewage solids which have been deposited by sedimentation.

SOURCES OF INFECTION
Places from which disease-producing organisms were acquired by the host.

SPECIFICITY
The limitation of a species of microorganisms to one species of host, or to at least a small number.

SPONTANEOUS COMBUSTION
Ignition of material by heat generated through its oxidation.

SPONTANEOUS GENERATION
The origin of living things from non-living materials.

SPORANGIA
Sacs in which fungus spores are formed.

SPORANGIOPHORE
A stalk that produces a sporangium.

SPORANGIUM
A sac that contains spores, usually numerous and indefinite in number.

SPORE
1. A simple reproductive body of a lower plant, capable of growing directly into a new plant.
2. Among bacteria, a thick-walled resistant cell.

STERIGMATA
Tiny stalks that produce spores at their tips, as in *Asper-gillus, Penicillium,* and mushrooms.

STERILIZATION
Killing microorganisms, usually by means of heat.

STOCK CULTURE
Cultures of microorganisms kept as a reserve for future use.

STREAK CULTURES
Cultures made by applying the organisms with a loop or other instrument to the surface of a medium, usually agar slanted in a test tube.

STRICK PARASITES
Organisms that require a living host.

STRINGY MILK
Milk that contains tough stringy clots as it is drawn from an inflamed udder.

SULFUR BACTERIA
Bacteria that use sulfur or hydrogen sulfide for food and oxidize it. Some forms store granules of sulfur in their cells.

SUPPURATION
The formation of pus.

SYMBIOSIS
A relationship between species of organisms whereby each receives some form of benefit.

SYMBIOTIC NITROGEN FIXATION
Nitrogen fixation by bacteria living symbiotically with higher plants.

SYMPTOMS
Functional disturbances brought about by diseased conditions.

SYNERGISM
The ability of two or more species of organisms to bring about chemical changes that neither can bring about alone.

T

THERMODURIC BACTERIA
Organisms capable of withstanding high temperatures.

THERMOGENESIS
Heat production by microorganisms.

THERMOLABILE
Destroyed by a temperature below the boiling point of water.

THERMOPHILES
Bacteria that grow best at relatively high temperatures, having an optimum of 55 C or higher.

THERMOSTABLE
Resistant to heat at the boiling point of water or thereabout.

TOXEMIA
A condition characterized by toxins in the blood.

TOXINS
Poisonous substances of complex nitrogenous composition produced by bacteria and some higher organisms.

TOXOID
A detoxified toxin that remains antigenic and can be used to confer active immunity.

TRANSMITTED LIGHT
  Light that passes through the object that is being studied with a microscope.

TRICKLING FILTER
  A sewage purification plant in which the sewage is sprayed onto a layer of crushed rock or similar material to provide an extensive surface for aeration.

TUBERCULIN TEST
  A test to determine whether a person or animal has been infected with *Mycobacterium tuberculosis*.

U

ULTRAMICROSCOPE
  A microscope that reveals very minute objects by the use of light that strikes them obliquely and is reflected into the objective.

UREASE
  The enzyme that hydrolyzes urea into ammonium carbonate.

V

VACCINE
  Anything which, if injected into the body, causes it to develop active immunity.

VARIATION
  The departure of the offspring from the parent with respect to some character. Usually more temporary than mutation.

VECTORS OF DISEASE
  Insects or other forms of animal life that transfer pathogenic organisms from host to host.

VEHICLE OF INFECTION
  Food or water containing pathogenic microorganisms.

VIRULENCE
  In bacteriology, the ability to produce disease.

VIRUSES
  Etiological agents of disease, typically of small size, most being capable of passing filters that retain bacteria, increasing only in the presence of living cells, and giving rise to new strains by mutation, not arising spontaneously.

W

WIDAL TEST
  The agglutination test for typhoid fever.

WINOGRADSKY TEST
  A soil test for fertility by determining its suitability for growing *Asotobacter*.

Y

YEAST
A kind of fungus which has been reduced to a more or less unicellular state by loss of mycelium.

Z

ZYGOSPORE
The zygote of certain kinds of fungi and algae, e.g., *Rhizopus, Mucor* and *Spirogyra*.

ZYGOTE
A diploid cell formed by the union of two haploid gamete cells in sexual reproduction.

www.ingramcontent.com/pod-product-compliance
Lightning Source LLC
Chambersburg PA
CBHW080324020526

44117CB00035B/2649